Who Will Rule the Future?

Huntington House Publishers

Huntington House Publishers

P.O. Box 53788

Lafayette, Louisiana 70505

1-800-749-4009

ISBN 0-910311-94-3

Library of Congress Card Number 91-55197

Printed in United States

Dedication

To Kristina and my son Paul—

I Love You

Contents

Foreword

Paul McGuire is an old friend of mine. He is also one of the people with whom I take genuine pleasure in having long, soul searching conversations. Because he lives in LA and I live on the east coast, our frequent discussions, via telephone, cost us a considerable amount of money! However, as anyone who reads this book will see, the privilege in sharing Paul's ideas is well worth sharing.

Paul McGuire is that rare combination of a biblically committed Christian and an articulate man of the world. In *Who Will Rule the Future?* Paul explores a wide range of topics with a precise eye for detail and a flare for a well turned phrase. In this entertaining and informative book, the reader will find a persuasive array of facts concerning the failure of the modern secular utopian experiment. It has tried, as Paul shows, to produce the "New Man" and has instead only produced moral anarchy.

With his imminent knowledge of popular culture, Paul McGuire leads us through the netherworld of "New Age" culture, politics, pseudo religions, false claims, and "enlightenments." He shows us that all that glitters is indeed not gold and that promises that we are on the edge of a "New World Order" ring hollow. In fact, as Paul writes, the real battle confronting our society is as ancient as the old serpent himself. Evil and sin cannot be wished away and replaced by a "new consciousness" let alone a "New World Order."

We Christians who wish to see our society abandon the folly of sin, and instead take the path of repentance toward Christ, will do well to read this book and let Paul McGuire help us see the truth of the situation that confronts our society—in other words, to see what is really important in what is going on in our world today. For as Paul writes: "Men and women act in accordance with some belief system. To fight only peripheral battles . . . without attacking the fundamental issues of a world view will not solve the problem."

It is to the fundamental issues that Paul addresses himself. He confronts the issues of basic psychic presumptions, issues of what the secular elite who now dominate our culture are really driven by, and issues of apathy of so-called Christians who have left the stage bereft of political, cultural, artistic, or any genuine historic witness.

Paul McGuire shows us that many Christians have reduced their Christianity to a mere subjective religious experience and in fact no longer believe that Christianity is Truth. A kind of "New Age" psycho-babble not much different from the false religions that the secular world has embraced, instead of authentic orthodox Christianity, is now very much in evidence in the Christian community. Apropos of which Paul writes: "Christianity as a religion is a weak opponent of our day, while Christianity as Truth can indeed confront our society and has the power to change it."

Paul challenges us to rethink our Christian attitude toward the world. He challenges us to be a positive guiding appearance in the world around us. Paul points out that it is not sufficient for Christians to be a "pietistic moral majority" standing in pharisaical judgement of the world. As he writes: "The world and the artistic community know what we are against . . . but what are we for?"

If the moral chaos that surrounds us is not to be allowed to devolve into a totalitarian climate of depression, if religious civil liberties are to survive, and if the Christian witness is to prosper, then we will all do well to give this book a serious reading.

Foreword

Paul writes: "The contemporary Judeo-Christian culture has made a fundamental error in strategy as it confronts the secular juggernaut." The failure is evidenced in the mangled bodies of the aborted babies that litter our landscape. This failure can be seen in the quiet but deadly erosion of Christian civil liberties. It can be observed in the false "Christian" church that often seems to be more akin to the entertainment industry than to genuine sacramental orthodoxy. Paul McGuire does more, however, than merely criticize failures of the church and the totalitarian impulses of our contemporary cultures. He adds startling and bright ideas to the Christian side of the current debate that is part of our cultural war.

I can only hope that *Who Will Rule the Future?* will find many readers who, through this book, will come to know an original mind and a daring Christian.

Franky Schaeffer
March 21, 1991

Acknowledgments

My thanks to:

Mark Anthony and Laura England at Huntington House Publishers for their commitment to this book

my wife Kristina for carrying my new son Paul and for her love and encouragement

the McGuire and David families

Reverend Jack Hayford and the Church On The Way

Franky Schaeffer for his friendship and wisdom

Chapter One

The Future and the New World Order

In a recent press conference the president of the United States, George Bush, repeatedly referred to the emergence of a "New World Order." The president was talking about the new economic and political order that is now emerging in the world. Communism has failed and a new global interdependence is growing between Europe, the United States, Japan, and the other nations of the world.

However, the concept of a New World Order is far broader than that. Our world is not only experiencing major shifts on the political and economic fronts; but now that communism and humanism have failed as workable ideologies for a changing world, a new philosophical world view based on a merger of Eastern mysticism and New Age ideas with science is dawning upon our society.

Ideas have consequences, and a powerful emergence of new philosophical ideas will radically affect the society we live in. Ultimately, the entire landscape will be changed. Thus, the economic and political changes coupled with new philosophical ideas will indeed produce a New World Order. As we move into this next millennium and the twenty-first century, we must say good-bye to the world as we now know it and be prepared for a New World Order.

Current events in the Middle East, the rise of a United States of Europe, global weather changes, and the fall of communism (along with the spread of New Age ideas) have caused Christians to view the unfolding of prophetic events such as the emergence of the Antichrist, Armageddon, and the Second Coming with renewed interest. However, despite endless speculation regarding the end of the world, a very real end of the world—as we know it—is already taking place on a far more subtle level. We are currently being engulfed by sweeping changes that are going to totally change the world we live in. These changes are not speculative. They are happening right now in government, industry, medicine, law, politics, media, and education.

While many people seem to be concerned with the rise of a super authoritarian leader, which the Bible calls the Antichrist, a very real spirit of Antichrist has already been unleashed in our land. The mark of the beast or the work of that spirit has already been made manifest in human personalities that have yielded and succumbed to dark philosophies (philosophies that deny the Son of God). This is not to say that we should not be concerned with prophetic events and signs of the last days. But if we are so concerned with future prophetic signs, we might miss powerful spiritual realities, which are equally significant and taking place all around us.

Furthermore, the personal, living God of the universe has not called us to fear concerning the rise of a New World Order and prophetic events. Instead, we have been called, as the people of God, to prayer, intercession, boldness, creativity, and intelligent activism. We are called to literally change the direction of civilization wherever possible by turning back the darkness and invading our culture with the light of God and evangelize the lost.

As modern Daniels and Josephs who prophetically saw the coming changes upon their society and did not succumb to fear, so we as true biblical Christians must resist the climate of paranoia and fear. We must move boldly to establish God's mandate for this hour. This mandate includes prayer, intercession, evangelism, ministry to the poor and homeless, political and cultural leadership, and media, artistic and creative leadership as well as solutions to the major problems of our day.

The key question before society in the next decade and the new millennium is "Who will rule the future?" We are currently entering into what has been termed a "spiritual Armageddon" and a major confrontation between opposing world views. *Either Christianity will re-establish its influence on the world, or we will slide into a new world order based on New Age and mystical ideas.*

It is great cause for alarm that millions of people do not seem to understand what is at stake. There seems to be a prevailing notion that "if we don't bother them, they won't bother us." However, history demonstrates that this is not the case. As the English philosopher Edmund Burke said, "The only thing necessary for evil to triumph is for good men to do nothing."

Like it or not, we are rapidly entering a brave new world. Daily events loom like road signs on the freeway indicating the direction we are headed: A united Europe, trouble in the Middle East, and the rise of the New Age. Recently, Yoko Ono's television special entitled "Imagine There's No Heaven" promulgated her late husband's (ex-Beatle John Lennon) belief in a one world government. Ono's special was televised to over one billion people on the planet. It was sponsored by the United Nations. The question is, do we see the alarming signs of a New World Order?

Battle Plan for the Twenty-first Century

We race into the new century to inherit a world produced by the choices we make now. America and the world is at a crossroads. The popular expression, "Think globally act locally" and an activism born of humanism mixed with mysticism alters our landscape forever. Where is the true biblical Christian agenda? Certainly it cannot be found in the tired old right wingisms with the cross wrapped around the flag.

What is needed is a new American and global vision produced from a biblical world view that will inspire and motivate a new generation to take the reigns of spiritual, cultural, and political leadership. The reason so many young people are experimenting with New Age ideas, Satanism, and radical ideologies is because the Church has offered them no vision for the world and for their lives beyond sitting in a pew.

In the 1960s and early 1970s there was a movement of political, spiritual, and social beliefs that captured the hearts and minds of an entire generation. Although many of these beliefs were built on very weak philosophical premises, the activists of this period managed to excite a generation. This energizing philosophical force produced music and films as well as political and social movements. Feminism, the New Age, gay rights, the sexual revolution, democratic socialism, civil rights, and ecology were all catapulted into the mainstream of our society from this period.

What is needed in our time is an authentic biblical Christian counterculture capable of catapulting a biblical world view upon society. However, at the present time this is not happening. Instead of a true Christian counterculture and a biblical Christianity that is creative and bold, we have what can be termed as "middle class American Christianity." This is not the same as true biblical Christianity. The reason young people, artists, and visionaries are rejecting Christianity is because they have not seen true Christianity. Instead they have seen a homogenized McDonald's hamburger, Pizza Hut, and Pleasant Valley Sunday version of Christianity; and they have rejected it. This American middle class version of Christianity is not powerful or visionary enough to compete with the New Age or even the humanistic ideologies of our day.

Contemporary Christians, whose values and priorities

have been shaped by the surrounding culture, lack real vision and commitment. They are often lifeless, predictable, and unable to compel the prodigal sons and daughters of our day to come back to their roots. The reason for this is that much of the contemporary Church does not understand who they are in Christ, and they have lost their own identity; therefore, they are unable to impart identity to others.

In reality, true biblical Christians are in a real, yet supernatural, relationship with the God of all the universe. They should be in the historic flow of what God is doing upon this earth and in this culture. The living God of all history is not asleep nor is He silent at this hour. God is immediate. His very presence is bursting with information concerning the solutions to the problems of our day. Ecology, world hunger, poverty, psychological wounds, disease and other adversities to peace and well being on our planet were never supposed to gain control over our lives. The personal, living God of the universe is omniscient and has solutions to these problems. God has the answers modern man is looking for if they would but ask and inquire of Him.

Mankind in general (as well as many Christians) is often disconnected from the Life Force of the universe, which is God Himself. In order for a new vision to sweep mankind and the Church, there must be a real reuniting between God and His people. When a person or group of people truly encounter the Living God of the universe their lives are changed forever by that encounter!

When an individual or a group beholds God, they are consumed by a vision of God. Therefore, once we understand God's goodness and purpose and have been filled with His Spirit, we will have been energized and empowered to transform society.

When God's vision has been imparted to an individual, he or she is completely transformed as in the case of Moses or the Apostle Paul, who had supernatural encounters with the Living God. There is a new generation rising that has had

such a supernatural encounter with God. This new generation has received a burning vision to transform our culture.
Alvin Toffler discusses this in his book *The Third Wave*.

> A new civilization is emerging in our lives, and
> blind men everywhere are trying to suppress it.
> This new civilization brings with it new family
> styles; changed ways of working, loving, and
> living; a new economy; new political conflicts;
> and beyond all this an altered state of conscious-
> ness as well. Pieces of this new civilization exist
> today. Millions are already attuning their lives to
> the rhythms of tomorrow. Others terrified of the
> future, are engaged in a desperate, futile flight
> into the past and are trying to restore the dying
> world that gave them birth.

> The dawn of this new civilization is the single
> most explosive fact of our lifetimes.[1]

An Agenda for Leadership

Who will provide the cultural leadership as we race into
the twenty-first century and beyond? Will it be those with a
secular humanistic/New Age-Eastern mystical world view?
Or will it be those with a truly biblical world view who are
able to provide pragmatic, rational and yet supernatural
answers as Daniel did in the Old Testament?

Sad to say, the spectrum of evangelical/fundamen-
tal/charismatic cultural and social leadership in our society
has been along a very narrow and often predictable path. It
is simply not enough to suggest that we are truly biblical
Christians. We must provide more than a limited moral
leadership that simply is *against* pornography, drugs,
abortion, etc. Clearly, as biblical Christians, we must stand
against those things (as in the case of Operation Rescue
whose bravery is evidence of a God-given mandate). Yet,
anointed by God in the power of the Holy Spirit, we must
take greater leadership in the full spectrum of life. This must

include art, film, literature, science, politics, theology, medicine, ecology, environment, social issues, psychology as well as the preaching of the clear message of salvation through Jesus Christ and His power to heal, save, and deliver.

What is needed is a generation of powerful Christians who, like the prophet Daniel, can assume a new role of leadership. This whole concept of a Christian cultural ghetto is anathema to the clear teachings of Scripture. True biblical Christians must become the heroes of our culture and our generation. God is not looking for heroes seeking a corrupt society's approval. He is looking for heroes who dare to establish the cultural mandate—heroes that are bold, creative visionaries and not afraid to look into the future and take it for the Kingdom of God.

A Titanic Turn in World View

A revolution in the consciousness of modern man is happening in our day. It will have profound effects in every facet of life in the coming century. Western civilization has turned to the East for answers. Eastern thought has affected everything from the production of automobiles to nuclear physics. Fritjof Capra, author of *The Tao of Physics* and *The Turning Point,* writes:

> The view of man as dominating nature and woman, and the belief in the superior role of the rational mind, have been encouraged by the Judeo-Christian tradition, which adheres to the image of a male god, personification of supreme reason and source of ultimate power, who rules the world from above by imposing his divine law upon it. The laws of nature searched for by the scientists were seen as reflections of this divine law, originating in the mind of God.[2]

What Fritjof Capra is talking about is a titanic shift in our world view that is going to have profound effects on every aspect of our culture. For once the basic idea (that there is a personal God in the universe) is replaced with the Eastern concepts of an impersonal energy force, then math, science, law, the family and all of society will begin to change. The nation of India is in abject poverty and has an oppressive caste system precisely because of its Eastern mystical world view. The foundational tenets of the Western world were built on Judeo-Christian beliefs. These beliefs are crumbling before a new mysticism that will have a myriad of effects on the way we live. Eastern mystical ideas about passivity and karma are summed up in the words "go with the flow" an expression popularized by Ken Kesey (author of *One Flew Over The Cuckoo's Nest*), and then pumped into mass culture through music with groups like The Grateful Dead. This concept of "going with the flow" or Paul McCartney's "Let It Be" is Eastern mysticism that encourages passivity in the face of danger. It stems from Hindu ideas about detachment and produces moral anarchy through a lack of moral initiative.

Ultimately, much of the shift in world view will have the same effect upon our culture as Charles Manson listening to the Beatle's "White Album." He heard messages that were not there about murder, mayhem, and societal breakdown. This is not to say that all Eastern ideas are bad. They are certainly not. But, when you begin to throw the Judeo-Christian foundation of civilization out the window, you produce a society without any moorings. Culture becomes adrift in a sea of existential and mystical nothingness. Man is dehumanized and authoritarianism rears its head as a stabilizing factor to manage the resultant chaos. It is no accident that the Eastern cults, gurus, and human potential movements consistently produce authoritarian leaders. People gravitate to a kind of moral fascism just to find order in the nonsense in the same way that the sexually permissive move toward sadomasochism as a kind of perverse cry for fidelity and commitment.

Reebok Sneakers and Human Rights

I walked into the famous Mondrian Hotel on Sunset Blvd. for an Academy Awards party and fund raiser sponsored by Reebok—the running shoes company—in conjunction with the human rights organization El Rescate. Television news teams poured into the hotel to interview celebrities such as Paula Abdul, Rae Dawn Chong, Daryl Hannah, Rob Lowe, and political activists such as Tom Hayden. Rock 'n' roll music was played by Stephen Stills of Crosby, Stills, Nash & Young fame in what looked like a sequel to the movie, *The Big Chill.*

While the high powered executives from Reebok mingled in the crowd sporting tuxedoes and running shoes, you could hear the buzz of conversation all around you. It seemed most people didn't even know what human rights issue was being supported. All the while L.A.'s most fashionable restaurants were serving platefuls of sushi, crab, chili, lamb, and shrimp to the crowd.

The *Rolling Stone* magazine's philosophy, which seemed to permeate the event, was reflected in a new generation of corporate Americans concerned about ecology, the whales, human rights and other issues. Corporate America is now being run by the same people who demonstrated in Washington, D.C. against the Viet Nam War. These good people have one fatal flaw: a total naivete about the reality of evil and totalitarianism. Inheriting the Ken Keseyesque/sixties/Sgt. Pepper's Lonely Hearts Club Band philosophy of "go with the flow," these good intentioned people are ill equipped to deal with the likes of a new Adolf Hitler. They are the Earth Day types who seem to be completely enamored with the prospects of a global society.

People are expecting totalitarianism to rear its ugly head in the form of an angry dictator like Adolf Hitler. They falsely believe that they are safe because no openly identifiable madman has rushed onto the world stage. Yet, the dictator and totalitarian leader of the future will reflect what communications theorist Marshall McLuhan labeled the "cool medium" of television. The dictator of the future will not be angry or explosive. He will be a dictator who works well with television. The new mind technologies like Scientology, Est, or the work of someone like Tony Robbins could easily fall into the hands of an evil genius like Adolf Hitler. He would appear in our day, not like a screaming madman demanding that his followers shout *Siegheil*! (Hail to victory), but cool and compassionate with the persona of someone like Werner Erhard or Tom Hayden.

This blue jean baby queen, sixties idealism that dominates a new generation is the very philosophical force that can potentially pave the way for a new kind of totalitarianism. The survivors of the holocaust who have tattoos on their arms and went through the death camps of Germany understand how quickly a political rally and new ideas can turn into oppression. Sadly, the sixties generation is not prepared for the coming totalitarianism, on the contrary, the "Let it be philosophy" has not only paved the way, but has ensured its arrival.

The French Revolution and the Problems of Globalism and the New World Order

Ultimately, the social activists and those who subscribe to the tenets of the Humanist Manifesto's I and II, either through direct allegiance or a compatibility of beliefs, are going to lead society into anarchy, chaos, oppression, and totalitarianism. These architects of a "brave new world" built by a so-called enlightened and invisible elite will foolishly usher in the greatest dictatorship the world has ever known.

It has been argued that the optimism of the French Revolution, influenced by the father of the Enlightenment, Voltaire (1694-1778), ultimately led to the Reign of Terror. Napoleon emerged as a dictator to rule through force and impose structure on the chaos.

The problem with the French Revolution was that it was built upon a faulty world view and false philosophical base. Since there was no workable belief system to hold together the revolution, it disintegrated into anarchy and repression with over forty thousand people killed (including many of the leaders of the revolution).

Conversely, Voltaire attempted to imitate the earlier English Revolution in 1688, which historians call the "Bloodless Revolution." This limited the absolute power of the Kings. Voltaire wrote about this in his *Philosophical Letters on the English Nation (1733).*

However, the English Revolution was based on many of the ideas of the Reformation, e.g., man is sinful apart from God, and through faith in Jesus Christ man can be redeemed. The English Revolution did not subscribe to the perfectibility of man. This was a humanist ideal. Thus in the French Revolution, when political and social chaos resulted, men who were evil and bent on destruction rose to the surface because "reason" and a false belief in man's goodness is not enough to hold back tyrants.

Ideas have powerful consequences. People act upon what they believe and what they are taught. People who believe in absolutes and accountability to God do not need to be governed by a repressive police force. They are free to operate within the self imposed proscription of their own world view. However, people who believe that they are "god" ultimately have no restraints and anarchy, moral and political, always results. Thus, the French Revolution ended in bloodshed despite its noble ambitions.

To understand what happened in the French Revolution we need to understand that in the Renaissance the basic ideas of man's perfectibility and what could be termed modern humanism began to develop. The giant of the Renaissance was Leonardo da Vinci (1452-1519). He was the embodiment of the Renaissance man in that he was a chemist, engineer, painter, sculptor, musician, botanist, architect,

anatomist, and writer. Leonardo da Vinci anticipated the
humanist belief that man is just a machine. Yet, da Vinci
ended up in despair during his final years because his belief
in the divinity of man could not hold up as he confronted
life's spiritual realities. He was like modern humanists who
often   end   up   in   existential   despair   or   seek   refuge   in
non-rational philosophies, mysticism, or madness. Leonardo
da Vinci saw humanism's defeat.

In distinct contrast, the Reformation, although far from
perfect, led by Martin Luther (1483-1546), encouraged a
world view which believed that there is a God who exists
and that this God has spoken through His Word. Thus, man,
who is made in the image of God, has a true reason for living
and has both worth and dignity.

The French Revolution emerged from Renaissance
ideals, which led to despair and anarchy. The English and
American Revolutions sprung philosophically out of the
Reformation, which produced hope and freedom. Basic
concepts in the American Revolution such as the checks and
balances in our federal government and the Constitution and
the Bill of Rights come from a Biblical world view.

Later revolutions in history, such as the Russian Revolution, produced dictatorship and the slaughter of millions. In
fact, the French Revolution led to Napoleon emerging as an
elite to rule; and the Russian Revolution led to Lenin also as
an elite to assume control while the Christian based
American Revolution led to democracy and government by
the people.

Therefore, in our day, when elites and social activists
seek to re-order our society through the courts and by assum-
ing control through multinational corporations, tyranny is
soon to follow. The danger of humanistic philosophies such
as globalism, New Age concepts, and scientific materialism
is that like the earlier French Revolution they presuppose the
perfectibility of man and ignore the sinfulness of man's
human   nature   apart   from   God. Totalitarianism   always

emerges to restore order from the chaos. Whether it be the totalitarianism that will emerge from the school of thought begun by B.F. Skinner (who seeks to condition man like a pigeon) or the totalitarianism of elites who maintain an illusion of democracy, or the blatant totalitarianism of a Hitler, Stalin, or Mao, the result will be the same.

Therefore when we see the steady slide toward a New World Order built on the false premise of secular humanism, we need to be alerted to the danger that lies ahead. Human history warns us that we have been down this road before.

The Necessity of a One World Government

Even if I were not a Christian, I would understand that our world is heading toward a one world government. It is being driven by philosophy and technology. Mankind is terrified of a nuclear holocaust as we all should be. The only solution appears to be the creation of a one world governing body or a one world government. It will be a kind of super United Nations that will regulate international disputes, ecological concerns, and economic problems. Since Mikhail Gorbachev began the dismantling of the Soviet Union and released some control over Eastern European countries, the cry for a one world government has increased. Major multinational corporations like Pepsico, which is now selling Pepsi Cola and 7 Up in Moscow, are interested in creating new global markets. Things like nationalism and patriotism stand in the way of opening up these new markets. There are economic forces pushing for a new globalism.

John Reed is a key player in global interlocking economies. He runs the largest bank in the United States and perhaps the most powerful one in the world, Citicorp. With over $230 billion in assets and earnings of $1.5 billion, Citicorp is a major player in the world economy. John Reed is an intelligent man whose library includes such books as *Quantum Reality, The Triarchic Mind, and The Cosmic Code.* The magazine *Manhattan, Inc.* called Reed "an amalgam of scientist and New Age philosopher. . . . A mystic at the head of perhaps the most powerful bank in the world. . . ."

"Reed's globalism is not an American globalism," says Reed. "I don't think you can say that a poor American is somehow more deserving than a poor Mexican or a poor Bolivian. The dawning era will be globally interconnected, heavily democratic, heavily capitalistic. Citicorp will be a supranational corporation, banker to a global community, a world that we share with five billion people."[3]

The quest for economic globalism will continue to cause supranational corporations like Citicorp and major oil companies to tinker with nationalism in order to preserve their profits. Oil companies who are interrelated with OPEC and the Arab oil cartel are not going to be major defenders of a nation like Israel whose nationalistic interests fly in opposition to organizations like the PLO and other Arab oil money backed enterprises.

The Emergence of Globalism

We must understand that the concept of globalism is not intrinsically evil. From a humanistic standpoint and on a practical level, globalism would work if it were not for the fundamental problem of human nature and the reality of evil in the universe.

Although the philosophical impetus for globalism began centuries ago, perhaps at the Tower of Babel, the concept of globalism has gained momentum since 1929 when a Russian mineralogist V.I. Vernadsky wrote a book published in France entitled *Biosphere*. Then in 1938 Pierre Teilhard de Chardin, a theologian/paleontologist wrote *The Phenomenon of Man*. In his book, Chardin discussed a new world view and man's evolutionary evolvement on the planet. In 1956 Princeton University held a symposium on *Man's Role in Changing The Face of The Earth*. During 1964-1974 the International Biological Program was initiated to take stock of "the biological basis of productivity of human welfare" on planet earth.

Then there was the UNESCO Biosphere Conference and a multitude of ecological activism that produced the first Earth Day in 1971.[4]

Finally, the Club of Rome's famous report *Limits to Growth* published in 1972 and President Carter's *Global 2000* Report all contributed to the hysteria being generated by the globalists. In addition, the United Nations and a whole host of international organizations have been created that discourage nationalism and encourage internationalism such as North Atlantic Treaty Organization, Organization for Economic Co-operation and Development, Organization of Petroleum Exporting Countries, International Labor Organization, the Food and Agriculture Organization, World Health Organization and the International Monetary Fund.[5]

There are other groups such as International Union for Conservation of Nature, the World Wildlife Fund, and the International Planned Parenthood Fund. The latter clearly has an agenda promoting abortion, contraception, and possibly the reduction of certain racial and national population growths.

Most of these organizations have sprung up within the last forty years along with the rise in multinational corporations. It is here that public and private interests merge—a trend Kenneth Galbraith discusses in *The New Industrial State*.

The point is there are powerful socioeconomic forces that are pushing for globalism and the demise of nationalism. On the surface this might seem like a good thing. Who in their right mind would not want global peace, international cooperation, and a clean environment? The danger is that this push toward globalism is riding on a wave of materialism and secular humanism. So, for example, if Pepsico or the McDonald corporation want to open new markets in Russia, there seems to be very little concern about the persecution of the Soviet Jews or Christians as long as there is profit.

Once upon a time when America stood for freedom, e.g., religious, political, and economic, globalism would have been difficult; for how could a free country merge with a totalitarian one? However, now all decisions are made on the basis of political and economic expediency. A good example would be the Beijing massacre in China where students were gunned down. After the initial media outrage, there was a strange silence on the part of our government and President Bush. Nobody wanted to rock the boat, because there were important economic interests at stake. This is the real danger of a global order. Religious and human principles must be sacrificed on the alters of expediency. Yet, there are powerful, invisible forces at work that will attempt to create a global government. But at what price?

Aldous Huxley warns us in *Brave New World Revisited* that

> the society described in *Brave New World* is a world-state in which war has been eliminated and where the first aim of the rulers is at all costs to keep their subjects from making trouble. This they achieve by (among other methods) legalizing a degree of sexual freedom (made possible by the abolition of the family) that practically guarantees the Brave New Worlders against any form of destructive (or creative) emotional tension.

Democratic Free Enterprise—an Emerging Ideology

In a recent issue of *Futurist* magazine, writers William E. Halal and Alexander I. Nikitin wrote a joint article on the coming merger between the New Capitalism and the New Socialism.

Utilizing the underlying philosophy of synthesis, these two men claim that the best means of managing a nation and its economy would be through Democratic Free Enterprise. This is a merger between the best of capitalism and the best of socialism. The authors write:

"From a broad, historical perspective, these remarkable but realistic prospects seem to indicate that the long evolution of civilization may now be leading to a climactic point. History shows a tortuous but steady trend of aggregation into even larger social systems: from primitive tribes to cities as nations to superpowers. As the revolutionary force of information technology spreads to create a central planet, this trajectory should reach the next logical stage of progress: coherent, manageable global order that works—One World."[6]

Citing examples of American companies such as GM (which built the Saturn car by using a collaborative form of governance), the formation of the Microelectronics and Computer Technology Corporation (which has been formed by over one hundred competing companies to produce advanced state of the art computer chips), strategic alliances between automobile manufacturers like General Motors, Ford, Chrysler, Toyota, Fiat and Renault, European economic blocs and mergers between government and business, the authors make a case for this new synthesis called Democratic Free Enterprise.

Although activists like Tom Hayden of California have long called for democratic socialism, our current economic policy being dictated by the United States Congress clearly does not believe in capitalism any longer but this new synthesis. During the recent budget summit not a single program was cut nor were tax dollars reduced. What is emerging in our nation is this merger between a new socialism and a new capitalism in which the government grows continually larger in an uneasy alliance between the public and private sectors.

In theory, the concept of Democratic Free Enterprise sounds wonderful. However, the reality is that it brings a paralysis to the economy with increased government debt and taxation. In addition, it brings greater governmental interference into the private affairs of its citizens. Consequently, government becomes a big brother endlessly watching over the lives of its citizens. As with all ever expanding governments, a subtle form of totalitarianism will emerge. This can already be seen in the United States where individual freedom is continually restricted and the country is being run by an invisible and powerful elite who share a common world view.

Like Terry Gilliam's movie *Brazil*, our nation is being run by an invisible army of compartmentalized bureaucrats all in the name of something like Democratic Free Enterprise. Since the fall of the Berlin Wall, more evidence has materialized that communism and socialism are disasters bitterly resented by the people who had to endure them. Only from the halls of academia could a ridiculous argument for socialism now called Democratic Free Enterprise emerge.

War in the Gulf

The whole world was mesmerized as the first reports of the United States and allied European forces launched a massive air attack against Saddam Hussein. Only in our futuristic and satellite linked society could the entire world watch and hear as a high tech military war machine launched billion dollar Stealth Bombers, F-15s, and missiles at Iraq. Even as Hussein counter attacked with Scud missiles hitting Tel Aviv and surrounding areas, millions of Americans sat transfixed as terrified news representatives donned gas masks, and the streets of Jerusalem were emptied.

When the news that Israel was first hit by missiles reached the world, millions upon millions of people began to seriously consider the possibility of World War III and Armageddon—including the Fairfax district of Los Angeles where bearded Orthodox Jews gathered to pray. At the White House evangelist Billy Graham led the president of the

United States and his staff in prayer. The whole world turned to God as the final hope.

In addition, in offices and work places around the world ancient biblical prophesies of Armageddon and the end of the world were being openly and freely discussed by people who once scoffed.

It appears that the looming possibility of global catastrophe has produced a climate where millions are now seeking God for answers. They are re-examining the prophesies of the Old and New Testament. Secular humanistic and New Age philosophies seem useless in the face of apocalypse. Many are returning to a Judeo-Christian world view in times of crisis, and unprecedented opportunities for revival and evangelism are beginning to open during this planetary shaking.

Despite the echoes of Armageddon, there are still many who continue to stay in the stream of secular humanistic and Eastern mystical thought. These people believe that "end of the world" prophesies are dangerous and self-fulfilling scenarios that are being created by nations and individuals who, they believe, are unconsciously following an unnecessary map to destruction. These people believe that if we simply "give peace a chance" and unite in a one world government all will be well.

All We Are Saying Is Give Peace a Chance

As the possibility of World War III looms over the Middle East, there has been a revival of the peace movement of the 1960s. I was personally active in the peace movement and took part on the March To Washington to protest the Viet Nam War. I was also active in many other demonstrations. I understand first hand the sincere desire for peace.

The son of the late Beatle John Lennon, Sean Lennon, recently assembled a group of rock stars including Iggy Pop, M.C. Hammer, Tom Petty and others on Virgin Records to record an update of the song "Give Peace a Chance."

Sean Lennon stated that he did not believe that man had to annihilate himself. The lyrics to his song mention things like Armageddon, the HIV virus, and toxic waste. Sean Lennon's plea for peace is a noble one, and we all share his dream of peace. However, all these collective cries for world peace are philosophical upper story leaps. It ignores one cruel reality: mankind is a fallen creature with a sinful nature that expresses itself in global conflicts.

The humanistic ideal of a world of peace is impossible without the Prince of Peace ruling in men's hearts. What all the peace movements ignore is the fact that there are some men who desire power and conquest above all else; and they will manipulate governments, people, and political situations to accomplish their purposes. Saddam Hussein is such a man. The modern peace movements, built on the philosophy of men like Gandhi, presume that man is basically good; this is a false premise. Man is capable of both good and evil, but as a fallen creature, who has become sinful, man continually expresses in the world of morality, politics, and the physical universe, his darker nature. It is not until man's sinful nature is corrected through repentance that true peace can be established.

This is not to say that as both nations and citizens we should not do everything in our power to create peace. Diplomacy, cooperation between nations, economic sanctions and other non-violent means should always be a first option. War is horrible and should never be glamorized as patriotic or treated as a game.

The Hundredth Monkey

Higher consciousness advocate and teacher Ken Keyes, Jr., wrote a book entitled *The Hundredth Monkey* that has sold over a million copies. Keyes, who also wrote the Eastern mystical classic *The Handbook for Higher Consciousness*, tells us how particular species affect one another. In *The Hundredth Monkey* Keye's suggests that if enough human beings believe that there will be a nuclear war then we will reach a "critical mass" and create our own reality and a nuclear war will break out. On the other hand, if enough human beings believe in world peace, then this will become a reality.

This myth has gained increasing popularity. Dr. Wayne Dyer, author of *Your Erroneous Zones* and *You'll See It When You Believe It,* discusses the whole idea of "oneness" in the latter. Dyer talks about the invisible connection between species that physicists call "phase transition."[7] In this idea of "phase transition" scientists say that when atoms within a molecule align in a specific way a critical mass occurs. Once the critical mass occurs, a chain reaction takes place in which all the atoms spontaneously line up in the same way. Futurists like Barbara Marx Hubbard, Ken Keyes, physicist Fritjof Capra and Gary Zukav who authored *The Dancing Wu Li Masters* all buy into this correlation between consciousness and physics.

Basically, the idea is a pseudo scientific application of the "create your own reality" concept. Nick Herbert's *Quantum Reality*, Lewis Thomas's *Lives of a Cell*, Rupert Sheldrake's *A New Science of Life* and Richard Bach's *The Bridge Across Forever* all deal with these themes. One problem with this idea is that it ignores and rejects biblical prophecy, which talks about the reality of both the end of the world and Armageddon. In other words, no matter how much we sit around and think nice thoughts it is not going to deal with the reality of evil in the universe. The subjective idealism of Berkeley and skepticism of Hume is easily identified in the writings of these authors. Their denial of a reality, which exist independently of our cognitive process, is destructive both individually and collectively. The critical mass or *The Hundredth Monkey* Theory looks rather silly in light of the historical reality of the Third Reich.

Do these believers in "phase transition" really believe that the existence of Adolf Hitler was a product of the "collective subconsciousness" of the German people? Do they believe that the annihilation of over six million Jews was brought about by the collective mindset of a nation?

There are some very dangerous implications to this theory if it is allowed to play out to its logical conclusions. I have heard that Werner Erhard's Est course and L. Ron Hubbard's Scientology have implied that the holocaust was the product of the Jews creating their own reality. What absolute and horrible psychological and philosophical bondage to put people in. These ideas are really forms of madness put in mystical terms. This teaching of cosmic fatalism based on Hindu beliefs (that is their philosophical source) brought the nation of India to its knees. Its inhabitants are afraid of killing a rat, because it might be the incarnation of one of their ancestors. This "all is one" belief system is the religion of mass suicide!

Yet, this is precisely the philosophical direction our culture is going. People like Barbara Marx Hubbard, Ken Keyes, Jr., Daniel Ellsberg, Baba Ram Dass and others are organizing for world peace and the establishment of a New World Order based on these ideas. There is nothing wrong with the desire for peace and brotherhood. Every sane person should desire an end to nuclear war. Every sane person should desire universal peace. But, the question is, will these actions truly bring world peace or world domination by a global dictator? History has already shown us that many revolutions promised liberation and instead brought slavery. A revolution built on faulty ideas such as Marxism, communism, and a French Enlightenment minus Christian virtues brought about tyranny and bloodshed. Consequently, a world peace movement built on wispy concepts of "universal oneness" removed from historical reality is like building civilization on a thin layer of ice over a giant frozen lake. All the good thoughts and good vibrations of peace will not stop the ice from caving in when the weather changes or any weight is placed on it. Ideas have consequences; ideas always play themselves out in the real world.

Once a culture believes that a "critical mass" of people believing in peace can establish a new millennium of world peace, society is in danger. Notice that these same people believe in abortion and euthanasia. What do you think will eventually happen to the people that believe in biblical prophecy and Armageddon? It would not take much philosophical adjustment to suggest that these people who believe in Armageddon (biblical Christians) are endangering our world. They are obstacles to achieving the critical mass. Perhaps they should be removed in special camps and maybe even exterminated so that global harmony can be reached.

Does that sound far fetched? Not really, who would think that people could say "SAVE THE WHALES AND DON'T KILL ANIMALS" in the same breath with "PRO-CHOICE AND ABORTION RIGHTS"? Philosophical schizophrenia is the by-product of the whole collective subconsciousness religion, which is a religion of madness not truth. Christianity is truth. It is not a religion. It is true not because we believe it or wish it to be so. Just as mathematical relationships and laws do not require our mental assent to be true (2 + 2 = 4 even if you don't believe it), so the doctrinal tenets of Christianity are true (even if you don't believe them). Christianity is true because apart from whether we believe it or not, Christ rose from the dead in real space, time, and history!

Evidence for a New World Order

> "The completely organized society, the scientific caste system, the abolition of free will by methodical conditioning, the servitude made acceptable by regular doses of chemically induced happiness, the orthodoxies drummed in by nightly courses of sleep teaching . . ."[8]

An emerging New World Order is growing up all around

us in a subtle yet insidious fashion. Mistakenly, many are looking for a United Europe or a single one world government to signal the rise of the New World Order. These things will come. In fact, a United Europe is already here, at least on the drawing board. The notion of a New World Order is already being feverishly promoted here in the United States. A powerful elite have already gained control. Aldous Huxley had this to say in *Brave New World Revisited*:

> Under the relentless thrust of accelerating over-population and increasing over-organization, and by means of ever more effective methods of mind-manipulation, the democracies will change their nature; and quaint old forms—elections, parliaments, Supreme Courts and all the rest—will remain. The underlying substance will be a new kind of non-violent totalitarianism. All the traditional names, all the hallowed slogans will remain exactly what they were in the good old days. Democracy and freedom will be the theme of every broadcast and editorial—but democracy and freedom in a strictly Pickwickian sense. Meanwhile the ruling oligarchy and its highly trained elite of soldiers, policemen, thought-manfacturers and mind-manipulators will quietly run the show as they see fit.[9]

Does all that sound far fetched? This is precisely what has happened in America. During the last few decades a powerful elite has moved in behind the scenes to run our country. The theologian-philosopher Dr. Francis Schaeffer warned us in his book *How Should We Then Live?*

According to Dr. Schaeffer these changes will not always be conspicuous.

> We must not think of an overnight change, but rather a subtle trend by the leadership toward a greater   control   and   manipulation   of   the

individual. Of course, some might feel uncomfortable about this increased control and manipulation in a relativistic age, but where would they draw the line? Many who talk of civil liberties are also commited to the concept of the state's responsibility to solve all problems.

Schaeffer also warns that totalitarianism either from the Right or Left makes little difference. Both political extremes will produce the same result.

> At that point the words left or right will make no difference. They are only two roads to the same end. There is no difference between an authoritarian government from the right or left; the results are the same. An elite, an authoritarianism as such, will gradually force form on society so that it will not go on to chaos. And most people will accept it—from the desire for personal peace and affluence, from apathy, and from the yearning for order to assure the functioning of some political system, business, and the affairs of daily life. That is just what Rome did with Ceasar Augustus.[10]

This is what is happening in America, the constant slide toward totalitarianism while much of the Church sleeps in its pews unaware of the Goliath that is devouring them. Look carefully at our news media which continually distorts the news and takes an openly hostile stand toward anything Christian. Do you think that this is accidental? Look at the way our court system continually blocks pro-life legislation or anti-pornography laws. There is a powerful group of men and women who are now running our country. They have not received opposition from anyone. Tragically, Christians are looking for someone to stand up and shout "I am the Antichrist" when in fact the spirit of the Antichrist is rampant in our land. Nowhere can the spirit of the Antichrist be felt stronger than in the push for totalitarianism. It's important to realize that you just don't wake up one day living under a dictatorship. A totalitarian regime grows slowly and subtly and is produced by all the small choices we make that don't seem all that important—until one day all of our freedoms are gone. "Forget about national anthems, flags, passports and get into one family consciousness. That turns me on" (Carlos Santana, Musician).

Chapter Two

An Eclectic Force Energizing the World Agenda

Kindness of Dalai Lama

On 10 December 1989 the fourteenth Dalai Lama (the religious and political leader of Tibet) won the Nobel Peace Prize. His name is Tensin Gyatso. The Dalai Lama was born into a peasant family in Amdo, Tibet in 1935. At the age of fourteen he was officially installed as the Dalai Lama. He has had to non-violently resist the Chinese invasion of Tibet for over thirty years.

Over one million of Tibet's six million inhabitants have died as a result of the Chinese occupation. Long before Tiananmen Square the Chinese army has repeatedly massacred Tibetan demonstrators—killing hundreds just three months before the Tiananmen Square blood bath.

Out of this background the Dalai Lama has emerged as a major spokesman for world peace. He has enlisted the aid of politicians and businessmen such as Fred Segal, the retailing entrepreneur in Los Angeles, California. The Dalai Lama's teachings stem directly from Buddhism. He has made efforts to develop close ties to those in the scientific community, specifically in the fields of cosmology, psychology, neurobiology, and physics.

The Dalai Lama believes that Buddhism is not a religion but rather a science and can tie spirituality with science and politics. He believes in the principles taught by Mahatma Gandhi and Martin Luther King, Jr. He has developed the Five-Point Peace Plan to create an environment for world peace.

According to the Dalai Lama, "our century is very important historically for the planet. There is a big competition between world peace and world war, between the force of mind and the force of materialism, between democracy and totalitarianism. And now within this century the force of peace is gaining the upper hand. Still, of course, the material force is very strong, but there is a kind of realization or feeling that something is missing."[1]

Although stemming from an Eastern mystical world view, the Dalai Lama expresses more concern for the ecology of the planet than many who misunderstand the biblical world view as it relates to planetary stewardship.

The Dalai Lama and the Buddhist tradition have made tremendous inroads into the scientific establishment and the world peace and ecological movements. In fact, in modern times, both the peace and ecological movements have been influenced by Eastern philosophy and Hinduism/Buddhism.

The Players behind the Scenes of World Events

Now that communism has failed in the U.S.S.R. a new super power that might be called The United States of Europe is emerging on the world scene. Powerful forces are at work to unite Europe under a single economic and political community. Jacques Delors, the president of the European Community's executive commission is pushing for a single European monetary system and elections are underway under the Single Europe Act for the European Parliment.

The United Europe would have a population of 324 million and a gross national product of $4.46 trillion. This compares to the United States which has a population of 248 million with a gross national product of $4.86 trillion. Clearly, this would make a United Europe a major economic force in global affairs.

Some people believe that this rise of a United Europe is the ten nation revived Roman Empire. Organizations like the European Economic Community (EEC) are designed to build a borderless Europe with a population of 320 million consumers. Interestingly, a Council of Europe poster entitled "Europe—Many Tongues, One Voice" features a drawing of the ancient Tower of Babel. Lockheed Corporation has run a new ad in *Scientific American* entitled "The Tower of Babel and Systems Integration," which claims to be working against the "Babel Effect."

In the *Wall Street Journal* IBM ran an ad with skyscrapers coming out of the Tower of Babel entitled "1992 Now," which is the target date for European unification. The ad talks about a common Europe. Clearly, there are powerful multinational corporations and major players coordinating this effort. AT&T's new Universal MasterCard is promoted as One World One Card.

As world events change and we move into what President George Bush terms "the New World Order," the United States will no longer enjoy its previous position. Along with a United Europe, Japan has already emerged as a world economic force. In fact, out of the fifty largest banks in the world, only four U.S. banks made the top fifty and only one, Citicorp, made the top ten. While Japanese banks like the Dai-Ichi Kangyo Bank took over the top eight places with $384 billion in assets, Citicorp had only $208 billion in assets.

At a recent conference on the New Age movement author Tal Brooke used the phrase, "If you want to know who has the power just follow the trail of money." In this changing economic climate there is a powerful group of bankers, multinational corporations and political leaders that are re-shaping world events.

According to Pat Robertson's newsletter *Perspective*:

> On April 21-23 of this year, the Trilateral Commission held a closed meeting in Washington D.C. Among the members present were Giovanni Agnelli of Fiat; Gerald Corrigan, head of the powerful Federal Reserve Bank of New York; Yoshio Okawara, executive Advisor, Federation of Japanese Economic Organizations; Count Otto Lambsdorff, former Economic Minister of West Germany; Shinji Fukukawa, Senior Advisor to the powerful Japanese MITI (ministry of International Trade and Industry). In the group were the chairmen of international banks and corporations, key thought leaders, and a sizeable number of former U.S. and European government policy makers. (Pat Robertson's *Perspective* July/August 1990)

The point is not that one single cohesive elite is completely running the world with its octopus tentacles controlling everything. Instead, as Alvin Toffler author of such best-sellers as *Power Shift, Future Shock* and *The Third Wave* put it:

> The Third Wave gives rise to groups with larger than national interests. These form the base of the emerging globalist ideology sometimes called "planetary consciousness." This consciousness is shared by multinational executives, long-haired environmental campaigners, financiers, revolutionaries, intellectuals, poets, and painters not to mention members of the Trilateral Commission. I have even had a famous U.S. four-star general assure me that "the nation-state is dead." . . . Precisely as nationalism claimed to speak for the whole nation, globalism claims to

> speak as an evolutionary necessity—a step closer
> to a "cosmic consciousness" that would embrace
> the heavens as well.[2]

Thus, we do not see one massive organized conspiracy that controls everything as much as we see many smaller conspiracies moving collectively toward a common secular humanistic/mystical world view. This can give the impression of a single conspiracy. In other words, ideas have consequences; history moves along certain courses due to the collective mindset of individuals on our planet who move in common ways good or bad.

The Trilateral Commission

The Trilateral Commission is an international organization formed by David Rockefeller, Chase Manhattan Bank chairman, to influence not only the economic affairs of nations but internal affairs within the United States.

According to the Trilateral Task Force Report entitled *Toward a Renovated Economic System*, "The public and leaders of most countries continue to live in a mental universe which no longer exists—a world of separate nations—and having great difficulties thinking in terms of global perspectives and interdependence."[3]

The Trilateral Commission, originally formed to manage goals related to the economies of the United States, Europe, and Japan has as its members such people as former president Jimmy Carter, presidential candidate John Anderson, William Brock of the Republican Party, Zbigniew Brzezinski, Senator Alan Cranston, Senator John Danforth, Congressman Thomas Foley, Senator John Glenn, Philip Hawley of Carter Hawley Stores, Lane Kirkland of the AFL-CIO, Henry Kissinger, David Packard of Hewlett Packard, David Rockefeller, John D. Rockefeller, Paul Volcker of the Federal Reserve Board, Caspar Weinberger, and Andrew Young just to name a few of the influential business and political leaders. George Bush was a former member of the commission.

Trilateral Commission members could be found in great numbers in the administrations of Jimmy Carter, Ronald Reagan, and George Bush. Although the goals of the commission appear benevolent, there appears to be a great deal of national and international tinkering with the political process and economics that knows no allegiance to America. In addition, the guiding philosophy of the commission is based on a humanistic world view and is pushing toward a New World Order and globalism.

The Trilateral Commission is *not* a conspiratorial group in the strict sense of the word but a group of powerful individuals who flow together in a common world view, which often produces the same effects as if it were conspiratorial. In the book *Trilateralism* Jeff Frieden writes:

> Is the Trilateral Commission a conspiracy? No more than the laws of capitalism seek to conspire to assert themselves. The Trilateral Commission is the executive advisory committee to transnational finance capital and quoting Richard Falk, "The vistas of the Trilateral Commission can be understood as the ideological perspective representing the transnational outlook of the multinational corporation," which seeks to subordinate territorial politics to non-territorial economic goals [4]

What this means is that the Trilateral Commission (the voice of giant multinational corporations and banks) owes no allegiance to any nation. It bows only to profit. It is like a giant dinosaur that cannot help but trample over the lives of smaller creatures—it is the nature of the beast.

What emerges then with the Trilateral Commission is the organization of a super powerful and global organization whose apparent goal is to insure monetary profits between the United States, Europe, and Japan. In the process it ends up controlling the United States and global governments along with their peoples, not in an all powerful conspiratorial sense, but in the sense of an immensely powerful agency.

It was David Rockefeller and the Trilateral Commission that put an obscure peanut farmer-politician in the White House. His name was Jimmy Carter. Out of nowhere, Carter got a most favored status by the major media, which have on their respective boards of directors Trilateral members. Carter was the pawn of powerful interests who used his "born-again good ol ' boy" image to appeal to both conservatives and liberals.

After Jimmy Carter was elected, he stacked his administration with Trilateral members who controlled both national and foreign policy. A largely invisible organization with almost infinite wealth managed to control an election and a great deal of the key policy issues of the freest nation on earth. The question should be asked, why have the national media never done a major story on the Trilateral Commission outlining who their members are and how they have managed to usurp so much power in our country? What is really happening here is the emergence of a powerful and invisible elite. They are attempting to run our nation and world for our own good.

It is important to note that the men who are involved in the Trilateral Commission are primarily well intentioned men who see themselves acting benevolently in our society and the world. For example, I do not doubt Jimmy Carter's conversion to Jesus Christ. These are not evil men, they are misguided men who have rationalized their actions as necessary in order to protect the world for economic freedom. This is an important point to understand. One does a great disservice to these men by imputing to them some kind of dark and evil motivation. Nevertheless, innocent or not, these men do not have a sufficient world view to understand the totality of their actions.

What the Trilateral Commission does not understand is

that by pushing for internationalism and taking steps to deliberately reduce a sense of patriotism and nationalism in the United States, they are concomitantly promoting a one world totalitarian government.

Once the economic systems and technological systems are in place for global control by a powerful elite, this absolute power is going to be powerfully misused. Man, apart from God, naturally gravitates toward deification. He becomes corrupt in the process as did King Nebuchadnezzar in the Old Testament.

Therefore, in the words of trilateralist member Zbigniew Brzezinski, "a world information grid" is being built by constructing a unified global media with satellites, news networks, and communications technology. Trilateralists want to manage and control news information. This is a prerequisite to building a global society. By building such a global society on a deficient humanistic base, they are going to unwittingly end up creating a Frankenstein that will come and devour them. Noble ideas are not enough! History shows us over and over again how men who attempt to gain power by controlling the world end up losing power and bringing bloodshed and misfortune upon the world. Napoleon, Hitler, Mao, Stalin and others attempted to create their own worlds; but destruction always resulted.

As a word of warning, in all political elections we need to be aware that all is not as it seems. There are big players behind the scenes maneuvering national politics on the Left and the Right, Republican and Democrat. If, as many believe, Carter was handpicked by an invisible elite—the Trilateral Commission—and George Bush has close ties to the same organization, in all likelihood the same possibility may exist in the 1992 and 1996 elections. This really destroys the notion of America as a democracy. However, in order to keep their power, this powerful elite wishes to preserve the illusion of democracy.

War in the Middle East—Preparing the New World Order for a One World Government

Throughout the Middle East crisis and war, the president of the United States has continually used the term "New World Order" and has constantly appealed to the global authority of the United Nations. The war in the Middle East will create the political environment necessary for the further establishing of this New World Order. The increased importance of the United Nations, or a similar body, as the prototype of a one world governing body, should alarm every citizen.

There were two parallel streams emerging throughout the war in the Middle East. One is the unified forces of a United Nations led alliance. The second is the re-emergence of a global peace movement that is being used by the global media to magnify the fear of war and amplify the need for a New World Order and a one world government. Thus, the war in the Middle East is being used secondarily as the perfect reason to surrender nationalism, diminish the power of the United States, and push for our merger into a United Nations style New World Order.

Throughout the conflict in the Middle East, the importance of United Nations Secretary General Javier Perez de Cuellar and the U.N. Security Council was being played up by President Bush. In fact, some say that the ghost of President Woodrow Wilson hangs over the current actions in the Middle East. In 1917 Woodrow Wilson gained a congressional declaration of war against Germany. It was not to advance American nationalistic interests but to establish a new order. This would be an order in which all nations could live in peace and safety. In 1918 Woodrow Wilson helped create the League of Nations, the forerunner of the United Nations.

The question remains, will the war in the Middle East be

used as an impetus to diminish the sovereignty of the United
States and establish a New World Order?

Given the enormous coverage of the current peace
movement by the global media, a number of questions come
up. First, are people like Ron Kovic, the former Viet Nam
soldier turned peace activist featured in Oliver Stone's film
Born on the Fourth of July and actor Ed Asner, who recently
protested the war in the Middle East, being used to set the
political stage for a U.N. style world government? Second,
Cable News Network owner Ted Turner, whose lover is Jane
Fonda, has been giving inordinate attention to the peace
demonstrations. Is Turner using his media clout to promote
the peace movement?

Due to the fear of global war and fueled by mass media
coverage the world is steadily moving toward a global
government. In this philosophical flow the sovereignty of
any nation, including the United States, is viewed as a threat.
During the next decade there will be increased media
emphasis on lessening nationalistic and patriotic feeling in
the United States. This will include indoctrinating the next
generation into accepting the need for a one world government. If you watch MTV, you will see this as a major theme.
We all want peace and universal harmony. No intelligent
person buys the concept "my country right or wrong." However, it is incredible philosophical naivete to assume that a
global government will solve all our problems. Global
government will, in the long run, produce global
totalitarianism.

Who Owns and Controls the Mass Media

According to Ben H. Bagdikian, author of *The Media
Monopoly,* fifty corporations control what America sees,
hears, and reads.[5] In other words, Bagdikian alleges, it is a
handful of powerful men who run all the newspaper,
television, magazine, record, publishing, and film empires
in our nation.

As an example Bagdikian cites Exxon, which has two directors on the board of Citibank who sit alongside directors of Mobil, Standard Oil of California, General Electric, Westinghouse, General Motors, Ford Motor Company, DuPont, AT&T, IBM, and RCA. Here we see that both Westinghouse and RCA are controlled by the same people in interlocking directorates.

In fact, interlocking directorates control all of the media and major corporations in America. The Times Mirror Company in Los Angeles has on its board of directors representatives from Bank of America, Norton Simon, TRW, Kaiser Steel, Ford Motor Company, American Airlines, Colgate-Palmolive, and Carter Hawley Stores (which owns the large book chain Waldenbooks and sells the books published by the Times Mirror).

According to Bagdikian's research, "almost every major industry whose activities dominate the news—the leading defense contractors and oil companies—sit on the controlling boards of the leading media of the country." For example, The New York Times Company interlocks with Morgan Guaranty Trust, Bristol Myers, American Express, Bethlehem Steel, IBM, and Sun Oil.

The *Washington Post*, which owns *Newsweek*, interlocks with CBS, Allied Chemical, IBM, Ford Motor Company, Levi-Strauss, TWA, and Wells Fargo Bank. Time Inc. interlocks with Mobil Oil, AT&T, Xerox, American Express, Atlantic Richfield, Borg Warner, and most of the major international banks.

Gulf & Western owns Paramount Pictures and interlocks with other major industries. In fact, all of the editorial decisions and production decisions are controlled by a relatively small number of people across the board in the media.

Objectivity and fairness must be challenged when news interests conflict with business interests. A case in point would be how the major television networks and magazines cover Israel. If the means of mass communication are run by the same people who run the oil companies, then there is going to be a conflict of interest when oil companies have a vested interest in protecting the Arab oil producing nations of OPEC.

Ted Turner's Voluntary Initiatives

Ted Turner, the founder of CNN and Turner Broadcasting System, is an example of a well intentioned man with a social conscience that does not fully understand the implications of his actions. I was having lunch with a studio executive at the MGM Studio cafeteria when Turner walked through the cafeteria after just having bought the entire movie studio for its film library. Every head turned to watch this athletic business tycoon and media mogul cross the room. Turner, who bought the Atlanta Braves baseball franchise in 1976, is a whirlwind of activity. He first came to national attention after winning the America's Cup in his yachting exploits. He often comes on his own network for conversations with men such as oceanographer Jacques Cousteau and Carl Sagan.

However, in recent days Turner has vilified Christians with a vengeance, although he reportedly apologized for calling "Christianity a religion for losers." Turner's commitment to humanistic ideals remain unscathed. Ted Turner has become a humanistic Moses. He has created Ten Voluntary Initiatives to replace the Ten Commandments. They are as follows:

1. I promise to have love and respect for the planet earth and living things thereon, especially my fellow species—humankind.
2. I promise to treat all persons everywhere with dignity, respect, and friendliness.
3. I promise to have no more than two children, or no more than my nation suggests.
4. I promise to use my best efforts to save what is left of

our natural world in its untouched state and to restore damaged or destroyed areas where practical.

5. I pledge to use as little nonrenewable resources as possible.

6. I pledge to use as little toxic chemicals, pesticides, and other poisons as possible and to work for their reduction by others.

7. I promise to contribute to those less fortunate than myself, to help them become self-sufficient and enjoy the benefits of a decent life, including clean air and water, adequate food and health care, housing, education and individual rights.

8. I reject the use of force, in particular military force, and back United Nations arbitration of international disputes.

9. I support the total elimination of all nuclear, chemical, and biological weapons of mass destruction.

10. I support the United Nations and its efforts to collectively improve the conditions of the planet.

In reality, with one or two exceptions, there is nothing terribly wrong about Turner's voluntary initiatives. The problem is that they have no real moral weight. In terms of moral authority, Ted Turner as a humanist has nothing to appeal to except the good intentions of humankind. It is unfortunate that many people are taking these Ten Initiatives seriously. They are a terrible substitute for the Ten Commandments, which, if followed, would solve all of the problems the Ten Initiatives are attempting to solve. Men and women who love God and their neighbor are not going to pollute the earth, use force, create war, and ignore the unfortunate. However, man apart from his Saviour is sinful and in need of redemption. People did not keep the Ten Commandments, and they certainly will not keep the Ten Initiatives. For example, men in corporations know they are polluting the earth and poisoning people with toxic materials. It is greed and selfishness that exacerbates the problem of pollution. Yet, greed and selfishness cannot be solved with an appeal to the good intentions of the human race. If that were so, the problems would have been solved long ago.

Ted Turner's ideas are ultimately pointless precisely for the same reason humanism is. It rests on the mythology that man is basically good, and if given the choice, will do the right thing. This is not true, man is basically selfish although he may possess many good and noble qualities. He may be capable of great acts of self-sacrifice and love; however, at the very core of his spiritual nature apart from God man is sinful and in need of salvation. This is the tragedy of all humanistic ideals. They are built on a falsehood and inevitably fall from their own weight.

Abortion and the Media

In a truly commendable piece of objective journalism the *Los Angeles Times* had the courage to run a series of articles entitled "Abortion Bias Sweeps into the News." In this series, the *Los Angeles Times* concluded the following after studying major newspaper, news magazine, and television coverage for over eighteen months—this included over one hundred interviews.

> The news media consistently uses language and images that frame the entire abortion debate in terms that implicitly favor abortion rights advocates.

> Abortion rights advocates are often quoted more frequently and favorably than abortion opponents.

> Many news organizations have given more prominent play to stories on rallies and electoral victories that are pro-abortion.

> Columns of commentary favor abortion rights 2
> to 1 in most of the nation's daily newspapers.
>
> Newspaper and editorial writers are sensitive to
> First Amendment rights and Civil Rights except
> when they apply to pro-life demonstrators such
> as Operation Rescue.[6]

The *Los Angeles Times* research revealed that Operation Rescue leader Randall Terry was portrayed as a "former used car salesmen" by the Associated Press, *New York Times*, *Los Angeles Times*, *Washington Post*, and *Newsweek*. Faye Wattleton of Planned Parenthood is referred to as "relentlessly high-minded, telegenic, immaculately tailored, a striking six-footer with an aristocratic bearing." The point is that Wattleton, who heads Planned Parenthood, finds herself heroically placed on the cover of the *New York Times* magazine section and headlined in *Time* magazine while people like Terry get dumped on by the media. The tragedy is that even after the *Los Angeles Times* did this story on abortion bias in the media—nothing has changed!

The New Thought Police

The belief that the American media report all stories in a detached and objective way is a myth. Although the means of mass communication are not under state control, they are far from being fair and objective. The key word to understand in comprehending our media is the term *HIDDEN AGENDA*. Media conglomerates like the *Washington Post*, *Time*, *Newsweek*, the *New York Times*, ABC, CBS, and NBC have hidden agendas.

They do not simply report the news, they actively manage information, censor information, and manipulate images in order to promote those causes they espouse. For example, just pick up any issue of *Time* or *Newsweek* and examine what these magazines consider important issues and how they treat them.

In the 17 Sept. 1990 issue of *Newsweek* we see an article entitled "Once a Red Always a Red—For Birchers, No Peach" by Todd Barrett. The opening paragraph reads:

> Since the cold war is over, whom does the John Birch Society have left to fear? Plenty of people it turns out. From its perch on the extreme right, the group still sees an internationalistic conspiracy at work, bent on destroying national sovereignty and creating a world government.

Now one must ask the question, Why is the John Birch Society important to *Newsweek*? Clearly, this put down is for a reason. It is interesting to note that *Newsweek* takes the time to discredit them.

I personally do not believe in one single, cohesive conspiracy out to take over the world. However, for *Newsweek* not to report the activities of the Trilateral Commission and other multinational groups is suspect. It's not good journalism.

Right below that article is an article on Robert Mapplethorpe entitled "Are Five Photographs a Fair Test?" We see a *Newsweek* defense of Robert Maplethorpe comparing him to the master painter Peter Paul Rubens. To compare Mapplethorpe, whose art consists of homosexual acts and kiddieporn close-ups of boy and girl genitals, to Rubens is not news reporting—it is promoting a particular liberal cause while hiding behind reporting.

In both cases we see *Newsweek* as an activist for certain causes. A couple of months earlier we see the same thing when in the 25 June 1990 issue we see *Newsweek* subtly defending American flag burning, 2 Live Crew, and the National Endowment for the Humanities. It all culminates into a lecture from *Newsweek* in an article called "Tinkering with the Constitution," which admonishes us not to amend the Bill of Rights to protect religion or the flag. This isn't news, this is promoting their particular viewpoint. *Newsweek* is not alone. This is common among all the major media.

What we have in effect is what George Orwell wrote about in his book *1984*. "Thought Police" carefully managed the news to control society. It is clear that the mass media in our country are strongly pushing for certain causes that will promote a New World Order. The values of this order are in direct conflict with Judeo-Christian values. The danger is that millions of Americans are being led by their noses and don't even know it. A new culture is replacing the old one, and many are not aware of the consequences that will soon follow. Most Americans think that they are "free thinkers" but in reality they think the way they have been programmed to think by a powerful elite.

> With an elite providing arbitrary absolutes, not just TV but the general apparatus of the mass media can be a vehicle for manipulation. There is no need for collusion or a plot. All that is needed is that the world view of the elite and the world view of the central news media coincide. One may discuss if planned collusion exists at times, but to be looking for the possibility of a clandestine plot opens the way for failing to see a much greater danger: that many of those who are in the most prominent places of influence and many of those who decide what is news do have the common, modern, humanist world view.[7]
> (Francis Schaeffer)

The Hidden Agenda to Change the Constitution

In the United States there is an elite political and intellectual minority who have been unable to gain popular and democratic support for their plans to re-order American society. As such, they have gone underground and have attempted to radically re-construct the United States through a kind of legal activism. They have used the courts to force change upon the American public largely against their free will.

A case in point would be that of Judge Robert H. Bork who was nominated by Ronald Reagan to the Supreme Court. Judge Bork had impressive legal credentials. He taught law at Yale law school and was Circuit Judge on the U.S. Court of Appeals for the District of Columbia. However, as a staunch defender of the Constitution of the United States, he was the subject of an all-out attack by those who have a hidden liberal agenda in our nation.

Senators Biden, Kennedy, and Metzenbaum, the American Civil Liberties Union, People for the American Way, Planned Parenthood, the National Women's Law Center, the National Organization for Women, the Feminist Men's Alliance, Ralph Nader's Public Citizen Litigation Group, the AFL-CIO and many others organized to keep Robert Bork off of the Supreme Court.

According to Bork, "It is important to understand the degree which the charges were leveled against me during the confirmation battle were false and known to be so by those who made them. That is so because, in the struggle for dominance in the legal culture and in the general culture, this episode is a revealing case study."[8]

Robert Bork points out that this case merely illustrates the larger battle for the control of the culture and the courts of the United States by a activist/humanist minority who cannot gain popular control through elections by the consent of the people. These activists are attempting to force the people, through the enactment of law, to accept the re-ordering of society based on the humanist agenda.

Robert Bork states:

> They are relentlessly disingenuous in advancing their agenda. In the guise of "protecting our civil rights," an idea that most Americans approve, they urge the courts to adopt as "civil rights" positions on a host of controversial

issues, that in fact divide public opinion and are
nowhere found in the Constitution or the statutes
of the United States—and which in fact, the
American people will not allow their legislators
to enact.

Bork's words expose the myth that groups like People
for the American Way and the ACLU are even remotely
interested in the rights of the people or the American way.
These groups are wolves in sheep's clothing who are attempting to force their will and vision for America while
hiding behind the facade of protecting the people's civil
rights.

These people are out to completely alter the fabric of the
American way of life. However, in order to do so they must
first alter and rewrite the Constitution of the United States.
They had to stop Bork because he had the dangerous legal
knowledge that could expose the fact that what they were
doing was changing the Court and the Constitution to fit their
agenda.

According to Bork,

> The public campaign, designed to influence
> senators through public opinion polls, con-
> sisted of systematic distortion of my academic
> writings and judicial record. . . . The ferocity of
> the attack. . . . The ideological stance of the
> assailants, and the tactics they used all showed
> that the opposition knew they were fighting over
> more than one judge. They were fighting for
> control over the legal culture. They knew that in
> reality and perhaps even more important, sym-
> bolically, they must defeat a nominee who had
> for long expressed in writing the philosophy of
> original understanding [of the Constitution] and
> had tried to show the lack of foundation for the
> liberal culture's most important victories.[9]

The disturbing thing is that the vast majority of

Americans do not have even the foggiest notion of what is happening in our nation and, sad to say, a large segment of the Christian community remains dangerously uninterested in the basic issues which affect their personal and religious freedoms directly.

What is happening is the steady erosion of our basic constitutional freedoms by an activist minority that is using the courts of our nation to force their will upon us whether we like it or not.

Big Business and Babylon

> For all the nations have drunk of the wine of the passions of her immorality, and the kings of the earth have committed acts of immorality with her, and the merchants of the earth have become rich by the wealth of her sensuality. (Rev. 18:3—NAS)

In America gross sexual immorality is financed through and merged with big business. That's why neatly coiffured business executives, and many of them probably church goers, finance the pornography industry. Let's take one example out of many. The troubled Spectradyne Inc., is the leading provider of adult channels in hotels. Although, Spectradyne may soon merge with another company such as Comstat Video Enterprises, it is a classic example of how big business is in bed with the pornography industry.

Spectradyne Inc., is primarily in the business of mainstreaming adult pay-per-view movies into hotel rooms across America. According to the *Los Angeles Times*, "Spectradyne's $440 million of debt includes $240 million in credit lines from a group of banks led by Wells Fargo, $125 million in reset notes and $75 million in subordinate debentures."[10] In other words, American banks and investment companies are bankrolling pornography. Ironically, the hundreds of millions of dollars that this one pornography distributor spends on adult fare far exceeds the annual operating budgets of Christian evangelistic organizations, which the mass media constantly rail about.

Billionaires Marvin Davis and Robert M. Bass have been involved in the transactions, and Spectradyne is available on the stock exchange. Furthermore, Spectradyne is available in 670,000 hotel rooms in the United States while Comstat Video Enterprises is available in 300,000. This adult fare is available in Hilton, Marriot, and Sheraton hotels with future markets in hospitals and overseas hotels. It is interesting to note how comfortably American business merges with pornography.

However, it doesn't stop there. The *Los Angeles Times* reports on what is termed "tasteful pornography." With Dennis Hunt's article entitled "Feminine Porn Finds a Niche in Marketplace" or "What's New in Home Video" which begins, "A video store is a great place to go if you want to see sharp contrasts side by side. Within just a few feet are not only love and war, drama and comedy but also children's videos and X-rated tapes."[11] It's not exactly that the *Los Angeles Times* endorses pornography, it's just that they appear to legitimize it. Contrast their article on pornography with most articles on evangelism, which is extremely critical. The idea is that pornography, if "tasteful," is okay. Ahhh! That word tasteful is the key word. What then is tasteful? Displaying the *Story of O* which is an S & M saga or *Deep Throat* next to *The Little Mermaid*? Is that tasteful? That's what's really going on in most video stores—X-rated fare ten feet away from children's videos.

The onslaught of unbridled hedonism has just begun. MTV, that bastion of Judeo Christian values and vigorously defended by that great intellectual Frank Zappa, who brought us Suzie Creamcheese and the Mothers of Invention, has soft porn music videos of Madonna chained nude in bed, Cher in a body stocking with masking tape, or Billy Idol re-doing Jim Morrison's "L.A. Woman" with a nun french kissing the ear of Idol and then lying on a bed in stockings. The Playboy

Channel, which provides the first amendment rights of artistic expression of women masturbating and the soon to be released "Hot Rocks," which will be rock videos with near or full frontal nudity, is only the beginning.

If European television is the precursor to American television, then we are going to see soft core commercials, adult soap operas with full frontal nudity, and eventually sexual acts along with increasing sexually explicit content at every level. Already homosexual soap operas are on the drawing boards and there is a storm of protest over Philip Kaufman's latest movie *Henry and June*. It features lesbian and homosexual love scenes and received the first NC-17 rating.

Ironically, the American Newspaper Publisher's Association held a convention with *Futurist*'s Alvin Toffler; John Seely Brown of Xerox Corporation; and Michael D. Eisner, the chairman of Walt Disney Co. They asked the question, "Where is technology leading American society? Is it increasingly fragmenting the nation, breaking down the social institutions . . .?"

Chapter Three

The Invisible Realm

Science and the Invisible Realm

Modern physics and mathematics have now postdated, what can be termed, parallel reality. In other words, in addition to the world of our physical senses, there is a parallel universe in another dimension that exists simultaneously. Thinkers of antiquity wrote about this dimension: Socrates, Plato, Aristotle, etc.; but beginning with the materialism of Hobbes, this dimension was denied.[1] The Bible calls this invisible realm the spiritual world.

Much of modern science, which is steeped in the bankrupt philosophy of scientific materialism, would not identify this parallel universe as being a "spiritual world." There is, however, a growing number of scientists who are attempting to merge science and Eastern mysticism. They believe in a spiritual world that can be proven by using mathematical formulas as well as new data.

In their book *New World New Mind*, Robert Ornstein, president of the Center for the Study of Human Knowledge and Paul Ehrlich, professor of Biological Sciences at Stanford University, write in an imaginary news piece.

> Do you think you see the real world? . . . Bats put together their picture of the world from the echoes of their squeaks; electric fishes by perceiving distortions in electrical fields that they

themselves create. These worlds are just as real
as ours. We, too, have a highly selective view of
the world. Our sensory systems emphasize
what's going on in a narrow band of electromag-
netic spectrum of energy—that is, we "see"
things. Always remember that our view of the
world is biased by man things, not the least of
which are the limitations of the sense organs we
have evolved.[2]

Ironically, these scientists are part of what can be called,
"The New Science" which is a powerful movement within
the scientific community that no longer accepts a merely
materialistic view of the universe.

The Nature of Conflict in More Than One Dimension

Once we understand that our physical universe is just
one layer of reality that is perceived with our physical senses,
we can fully comprehend what the Scriptures say about the
existence of a spiritual realm in which a great conflict is
being played out.

If we are not careful, we can fall into the trap of believing
that life and spiritual conflict is relegated to the material
world. Subtly, we can adopt a materialist world view even
though we may say that we believe in a supernatural
universe.

We must understand that this great "Civil War" of our
day for values and beliefs in both the political and social
arenas is just one layer of a visible and invisible conflict that
is taking place. It is taking place, not only in the three
dimensions of our physical world, but simultaneously in a
fourth dimension as well.

Two inherent dangers exist in understanding the nature
of multi-dimensional conflict. First, we can over spiritualize
the conflict through pietism and develop a super spiritual
outlook that goes beyond what the Bible teaches in which
the physical world becomes less important than the spiritual

world. This is not true, and in reality it is part of the Gnostic tradition. It is not Biblical. And much destructive thought emerges from this error. This danger seems especially prevalent in the "charismatic" movements, which sometime over emphasize the supernatural. In some quarters they go beyond what the Bible teaches. The result is that the proper mannishness of man is lost and things like art, history, romantic love between husband and wife, science, work, politics, nature and the like are completely ignored. This denies to us the enrichment of a whole life well lived—the kind of life God wants for us.

The second danger is, of course, to either completely ignore the reality of the supernatural universe, or to diminish its importance. The result is that the importance of the physical world is over emphasized. This error prevents us from understanding how the reality of the invisible realm integrates with the physical world especially in relation to spiritual conflict. There is a tendency to ignore or de-emphasize things like the demonic realm, principalities and powers, and so on. If it cannot be known in the same way that bodies and their motions are known, it therefore does not exist—is the classic non sequitur argument of the materialists.

The Bible teaches us that life on earth consists of both what can be seen and what cannot be seen. The visible and the invisible. So we must understand that in regard to every conflict here on earth there is a spiritual side or component. When we look at the rise of Adolf Hitler, the rise and fall of communism, the spread of secular humanist thought, and the resultant chaos and social breakdown in society, or the spread of Eastern mystical or occult beliefs, we must recognize that they are physical manifestations of a warfare that is occurring in the invisible realm. When engaged in a warfare for values and beliefs, we must wage the war on every battlefield that it is being fought on in the universe. This means fighting the battles both in the visible realm and in the invisible realm. To ignore either battlefield, visible or invisible, is to lose the battle in that area of life.

This all too often is the great mistake of those who have held a Judeo-Christian world view. For they have ignored either one battlefield or the other in their fight to reclaim society and thus were not as effective as they could have been.

We must understand that philosophies, belief systems, mystical ideas, sexual practices, political machines, governments and prevailing attitudes are anchored in the invisible realm. In other words, they are energized in the fourth dimension in much the same way a film projector throws a movie up upon a movie screen. If we do not like the movie that is being played in our time, throwing tomatoes and eggs at the screen is not going to do much good. We must get to the heart of the matter. We must get to the spiritual source behind the image that has created the film. We must get behind the celluloid that is projecting the reality we call a movie or, as in the case of this analogy—life itself!

Many of the things we are fighting such as pornography, the occult, corrupt political systems, secular humanistic philosophies, drugs, poverty and the like are being energized from the fourth dimension. They must be dismantled in the fourth dimension through prayer, praise, and intercession. Then the business of waging war in the physical realm must happen with the nitty-gritty practical issues of life—participating in democracy, voting, organizing, demonstrating, and the practical application of intelligently leading a culture by developing workable plans. Christians have been inveigled into believing that they should not be involved in such activity. We have retreated from society and our retreat has created a vacuum. The secular humanists have been happy to fill that vacuum. Our children will pay a heavy price if we refuse our mandate to "be the head and not the tail." We must quit retreating and confront the enemies of God in an intelligent manner.

Understanding the Invisible Realm

Modern man has been taught that reality consist of what can be observed through the physical senses like seeing, touching, hearing, smelling, and tasting. However, there are realities that transcend the physical senses. For example, wherever you are reading this book there are numerous radio and television waves permeating through the atmosphere around you. You cannot perceive these signals through your physical senses. Yet, if you had a television or radio, you could pick up visual and auditory programs like MTV or "CBS News." This is a primitive and somewhat limited example of how things like television and radio signals can exist beyond our physical senses. There are entire worlds that exist all around us in another dimension. These realities exist beyond our physical senses.

Our physical senses give us information about a three dimensional world consisting of length, width, and depth. But, scientists recognize there are other dimensions—time and space. In fact, there is a fourth dimension of the invisible realm which is the spiritual world. This invisible realm or spiritual world exists all around us and affects everything in our physical world.

To limit your belief of reality to what you can perceive with your physical senses is very foolish. There is a parallel universe all around us in the invisible realm that measurably affects the physical world.

Human beings and animals live in the physical world here on planet Earth. Simultaneously, all around us in another dimension called the invisible realm there exist what the Bible terms angels, demons, Satan, and God in the spiritual world. Does that sound archaic or superstitious or like the subject of Dante's *Inferno* or a medieval painting? Some would say modern man has transcended such superstitious beliefs through science and psychology. Science and psychology based on the philosophy of materialism do not give adequate answers to the existence of the invisible realm. This has given rise to the new psychology and science, which affirms the existence of other realities.

The famous psychologist William James said that "our normal waking consciousness is but one special type of consciousness: whilst all about it, parted from it by the filmiest screens there lies a potential form of consciousness entirely different.... No account of the universe in its totality can be final which leaves these other forms of consciousness quite disregarded."[3]

William James was talking about the existence of an invisible realm that could be perceived through techniques of higher consciousness or altered states of consciousness. Aldous Huxley, the philosopher who wrote the novel *Brave New World*, suggested the same thing in his book *Heaven and Hell— The Doors of Perception*. In this book Huxley contended that by using psychedelic drugs you could go through the Doors of Perception into the invisible realm. The famous rock 'n' roll group The Doors, with lead singer Jim Morrison, coined the name of their group from Huxley's "Doors of Perception." Through the influence of Aldous Huxley, William James, and others, much of science has come full circle and now believes in an invisible realm. It is no accident that LSD prophet Timothy Leary, who coined the phrase, "Tune In, Turn On and Drop Out" was a former Harvard professor of psychology. His psychological evaluation tests are still being used around the country. His associate Dr. Richard Alpert advocates the use of drugs and/or mysticism in order to enter the world of the so called Higher Consciousness.

The point is that modern science now believes in another reality or an invisible realm. The question is, what is the nature and purpose of this invisible realm and what or who inhabits it?

Unlike modern mysticism and science, the Bible is very clear that in the invisible realm there is good as well as evil.

Thus, techniques of higher consciousness through meditation or drugs do not take into account the true nature of the
invisible realm and the real conflict between God and Satan.
This kind of tampering can place people in serious danger,
and often the unsuspecting become embroiled in the spiritual
world at the mercy of demonic influence. This is why the
practice of meditation or the use of certain drugs can
sometimes lead to demonic oppression, suicide, or mental
breakdowns.

The Bible and modern science, as well as mysticism,
share the common perception that reality transcends the
physical world. The Bible, modern science, and mysticism
disagree on the composition of this invisible realm. Paul
discusses this issue in the book of Ephesians.

> For our struggle is not against flesh and blood,
> but against the rulers, against the powers,
> against the world forces of darkness, against
> the spiritual forces of wickedness in the heavenly
> places. (Eph. 6:12)

The Apostle Paul warns of a supernatural conflict in
"heavenly places" or the invisible realm. Unlike the New
Age view that sees the invisible realm as basically a good
place, the biblical view warns that there is a great conflict
going on in the universe. It is being fought on earth and the
invisible realm.

The Relationship to the Spiritual Dimension and the New World Order

One cannot view history in merely naturalistic terms.
History is not merely the by product of human action and
human ideas. Although it cannot be seen with the naked eye
or necessarily measured scientifically, all of history has a
spiritual component. When we observe the flow of history
in our day, we must understand that the current direction of

both political and social forces are not solely determined by what can be seen.

Karl Marx wrongly attempted to reduce all of history to a class struggle. This totally materialistic world view ignored the larger realities at work in the universe. When we talk about issues such as globalism, one world governments, the battle for good and evil, the New Age, etc., we cannot put things in tidy little compartments labeled good and bad or God and the devil as some have done. We cannot simplistically reduce mankind or history into tidy little categories. History is marvelously complex, rich, and enigmatic. As mortals bereft of God's omniscient perspective, we cannot dogmatically examine human history and make offhand judgements. This is not to say that we cannot have true discernment.

Many conservatives and Christians have often looked at current events and history and have attempted to make overly simplistic pronouncements. This has discredited the one making them and the evangelical culture as well. Those who create conspiracy theories of every kind—whether it be a New Age conspiracy, one world conspiracy, Communist conspiracy, Trilateralist conspiracy, etc.—disregard the basic rules of intellectual honesty and jump to foregone conclusions that are either deficient, or false, or both.

When we talk of the existence of an invisible realm inhabited by angels, demons, and both the personal God of the universe and the devil, we are not attempting to reduce all of history to some kind of cosmic chess game between God and Satan. This naive view of history is at best one dimensional and ignores the immensity of the created order and certain theological realities. God did not create men and women as chess pieces to be played in a game. The problem with these conspiracy theories is that they end up reducing the immensity of a cosmic struggle to the level of a cartoon or comic book. The universe, God, and the devil are all far bigger than that.

History is gigantic, overwhelming, and powerful; it flows from the Dawn of Creation through the Fall like a huge river filled with all kinds of fish. It sweeps across all kinds of rocks and ponds. You cannot reduce the totality of history, which is interwoven with the infinite, into simple international conspiracies. First of all, God has not given any man or group that kind of immense power and control. History is littered with the debris of fallen dictators and schemers from the Tower of Babel to Communist Russia. It is within the providence of God to bring down and judge these empires.

The Scriptures very pointedly reveal that "our struggle is not against flesh and blood but principalities and powers." However, we cannot infer from this that every political decision or every action by a group is part of a satanic conspiracy. Men and women are led by their own ideas, vain philosophies, greed, and lusts. These may be influenced by activity in an invisible, spiritual realm; but I sense that often we over spiritualize history and assign to the devil and God what God has left to the exercise of man's free will.

Make no mistake that we are involved in a powerful, spiritual struggle between God and the devil—a great cosmic war if you will. But, we need to intelligently discern and biblically discern how, when, and where the outside forces come to bear on our present physical and political realities.

Too often in the evangelical culture an over simplicity and super spirituality emerges that attempts to make quick, shallow, and erroneous definitions that ultimately destroy the effectiveness and credibility of those making them. Nowhere is this more true than when we discuss the relationship between the spiritual or invisible realm and political and social reality.

The Satanic Strategy

The personal, living God of the universe is the great liberator of mankind. It is God who has broken the shackles of slavery through His Son Jesus Christ. Every good dream and aspiration that men and women have can be fulfilled in a relationship with the God of the universe. However, the fact of God's goodness is not readily apparent to mankind. There is a deceiver at work whose strategy it is to distort this and make it seem like God is the enslaver of mankind.

Distorting the truth concerning God's goodness is the primary strategy of Satan. He is the Father of Lies. It is a strategy that goes back to the Garden of Eden when the serpent tempted and deceived Adam and Eve. If we look at Genesis, we see the basic strategy of real evil in the universe.

> Now the serpent was more crafty than any beast of the field which the Lord God had made. And he said to the woman, "Indeed has God said, You shall not eat from any tree of the garden?" And the woman said to the serpent, "From the fruit of the trees of the garden we may eat; but from the fruit of the tree which is in the middle of the garden, God has said, 'You shall not eat from it or touch it, lest you die.'" And the serpent said to the woman, "You surely shall not die! For God knows that in the day you eat from it your eyes will be like God knowing good and evil."
>
> When the woman saw that the tree was good for food and that it was a delight to the eyes, and that the tree was desirable to make one wise, she took from its fruit and ate; and she gave also to her husband with her, and he ate.

Although there are some who erroneously believe that the account of Adam and Eve is a fable, in reality Adam and Eve were the real space-time genetic ancestors of the human race. In addition, recent scientific research into genetics and the DNA molecule indicate that mankind appeared to have a common father and mother.

In this historical account we see the fall of the human race from a spiritual and ecological paradise through a satanic deception that appealed to the pride of Adam and

Eve. First, we see the serpent in verse one begin to subtly question God's commandment, "Indeed, has God said, You shall not eat from any tree of the Garden?" Second, we see that Satan directly lies about the results of disobedience and tells them that God is trying to deny something good to them. In verse two he says, "For God knows that in the day you eat from it your eyes will be opened, and you will be like God, knowing good and evil."

In this passage of Scripture the adversary directly appeals to the pride of mankind by promising godhood to them. Adam and Eve were seduced by evil into doubting God's goodness and disobeying God's commandment. As history shows, Adam and Eve did not receive godhood when they ate the forbidden fruit. Instead, they brought about the fall of the human race by introducing spiritual death and physical death into paradise. The result was the rapid degeneration of Adam and Eve and the release of the death force or sin into the world. This separated them from a loving God.

As simple as this strategy seems, it is exactly the same evil strategy that is at work in our world today. At every point, Jesus Christ, the commandments of Scripture, and a Judeo-Christian world view are looked on as antiquated and somehow keeping man from achieving his or her full human potential. In fact, the entire Bible and God's message of salvation in Jesus Christ is under massive assault in our culture through the mass media, educational system, occult and New Age religions, and certain radical activist groups. It is falsely viewed as an instrument of oppression or, at the very least, a lower level of consciousness or social development.

The Battle for the Heart and Mind of Mankind

And even if our gospel is veiled, it is veiled to those who are perishing, in whose case the god of this world has blinded the minds of the unbelieving, that they might not see the light of the

gospel of the glory of Christ, who is the image of
God. (2 Cor. 4:3-4)

In our world today there is a literal battle going on for
the heart and mind of mankind. It is being fought between
the powers of darkness and the Kingdom of God. In our
global village culture, this battle is primarily fought through
ideas, words, film, records, books, and other media. In this
war of ideas, it is the images, impressions, and styles that are
often paramount to the exclusion of content. In our media
oriented world, it is the people who *look* like they know what
they are talking about who are given the center stage. True
content and knowledge are often secondary to appearance.

Unfortunately, the contemporary evangelical culture
often does not understand the media. Thus, Christians who
know the truth are rendered ineffective in our society largely
because of their lack of skill when it comes to communication. This passivity in relation to the media has been
produced by a non-biblical and pietistic theology that has
often been promoted within the evangelical culture and its
churches and learning institutions.

A quick overview of Christian media whether it be
television, film, literature, radio or music, would reveal, as
Franky Schaeffer put it, an "addiction to mediocrity." This
mediocrity in the battle for mankind may be what is causing
millions of people to reject Jesus Christ and the truth of
God's Word. It is a mediocrity that is directly responsible
for surrendering our culture into the hands of a real Antichrist
spirit.

Images dominate our culture: Madonna, the president,
sex, freedom, etc. Within this warfare of images, from which
people make moral and spiritual choices, we have the media
image of the Christian which is identical to the image of the
buffoon burned into the collective consciousness of an entire
generation. Now clearly, this negative image of the Christian
has been largely fostered and manufactured by people like

television writer Norman Lear of "All in the Family" fame who had a specific agenda to undermine the influence of Christianity in our nation. In addition, the direct prejudice by some in the motion picture, television, and news industries has done a lot to discredit Judeo-Christian beliefs in our nation.

Yet, perhaps the most powerful force to discredit the Gospel and Christianity has not been initiated by the enemies of the Gospel. It has been Christians themselves! Just look and listen to the landscape of Christians in the media, and discover an image of the Christian as an idiot being etched in the minds of millions.

Except for notable exceptions, Christian television can be a journey into the twilight zone.

Is this evangelism? Is this what Jesus Christ desires in our generation? Nothing short of a revolution in the consciousness of the evangelical Christian culture will create the changes needed to reach our world with the truth.

Here in Los Angeles the Church of Scientology, founded by the late science fiction writer L. Ron Hubbard, is very effective in using the media to win converts to Scientology. Now, please do not misunderstand me. I am not in any way endorsing Scientology by any stretch of the imagination. But, L. Ron Hubbard in some ways made a far better evangelist for Scientology than many Christian evangelists do for the Gospel. The reason is that L. Ron Hubbard was a creative genius that understood language, art, literature, and culture as well as how to manipulate images.

L. Ron Hubbard was a prolific writer of science fiction such as *Mission Earth* and *Battlefield Earth*. Hubbard also authored the best-selling book *Dianetics—The Modern Science of Mental Health* and he is the founder of Scientology. I definitely do not agree with the foundational tenets of Scientology. I believe they contradict the clear teaching of the Scriptures. It is clear, though, that L. Ron Hubbard knew how to communicate and win people to his cause unlike many Christian groups.

A recent full page ad in the *Los Angeles Times* Calendar section says "A culture is only as great as its dreams, and its dreams are dreamed by artists." It was a quote from L. Ron Hubbard along with a full page picture of him. In addition, major billboards all over Los Angeles have huge pictures of Hubbard saying "22 best-sellers and more to come." During Cable News Network's coverage of the War in the Gulf, the Church of Scientology ran a high powered ad for the book *Dianetics* that looked like a commercial for a big budget science fiction film. Interestingly, even after Hubbard's death, Scientologists manage to place his message on prime time. One wonders why Christian evangelistic organizations are not placing the Bible before our culture with equal boldness and imagination.

Unlike the evangelical Christian culture, which has often put itself in the position of opposing art, artists, and culture, the Church of Scientology wisely embraces our culture in order to win it. Recently, I visited the L. Ron Hubbard Gallery on Hollywood Blvd. just a few blocks from the Mann Chinese theatre. The gallery was a reflection of the mindset of the Church of Scientology. Paranoia was in the air as I walked into the gallery to get a tour. I was treated politely but as if I was a CIA agent attempting to infiltrate the organization. Yet, at the same time, the place was electric with energy and paintings that were the covers of Hubbard's numerous science fiction books. I couldn't help but admire the creativity.

I am not suggesting that Christians should not protest pornographic art; they certainly should. But, if the entire evangelical strategy revolves around denouncing popular culture, then it is doomed from the start.

The contemporary Christian culture has often defined itself by abjuring contemporary culture. It is unwise to base our identity on what we are against. Christians object to pornography in the arts. That is fine. But, what are we for in the arts? Where is the Christian voice in art and culture?

This is the problem in a nutshell. We are in a battle for the heart and mind of mankind on a global level. Yet, the popular non-biblical and anti-art stance of contemporary evangelical Christians is causing all efforts at real evangelism to self destruct.

Film director Franky Schaeffer says in his excellent book on Christians and the arts, *Sham Pearls for Real Swine*, "The church is now thoroughly divorced from its historic culture. While claiming to wish to reach mankind, it often fails because our culture cannot be reached from outside by outsiders who do not even bother to learn the cultural language."

Creativity—the Front-Line in the Battle for Mankind

One of the greatest errors in the strategy of the Christian culture is to minimize or dismiss creativity as the idle play of artists. This should be the front-line in winning hearts and minds to Jesus Christ. The Enemy of our souls fully understands the importance of creativity in compelling mankind to rebel from the living God and follow him. Yet, tragically the contemporary Christian culture rarely understands the importance of creativity; and as a consequence of this misunderstanding, we are allowing millions of young people to fall under the spell of the Dark Prince.

Communications theorist Marshall McLuhan coined the expression "The Medium is the Message." This phrase means that in our media oriented society the content of the message is secondary to the manner in which it is packaged and presented. People in our culture will judge an idea more on the basis of how it is presented than what the idea actually is about.

Just look upon the landscape of the mass media and observe how rock stars like Madonna, Cher, LaToya Jackson, Prince and the others are packaged. Most of these rock

'n' roll stars represent hedonism, rebellion, and self centered
values. This is not a prudish reaction to the music industry,
it is an accurate observation. Madonna lashes out against
moralists in her interviews and shouts four letter words to
her audiences; Cher wears little more than a transparent body
stocking and a piece of masking tape; LaToya Jackson rips
off her blouse in an MTV award ceremony, and Prince exalts
sexual promiscuity. Yet, these are the media role models of
a new generation.

Conversely, the religious media is, with a few notable
exceptions, unsophisticated when it comes to packaging
biblical truth with any compelling artistic force. Generally
speaking, religious broadcasters are not transforming our
society; they are basically entertaining a narrow audience of
Christians who are willing to fund such programming.

Due to the false theology of non-biblical pietism, the
Christian culture has expelled the artist and visionary from
its midst. We should not be surprised to find that the artist
and visionary in our culture bitterly resent Christians whom
they view as repressive fundamentalists. As a reaction they
are striking back with force at the Christian culture through
art, film, literature, and television.

There is a place for protest against art, film, and
television. Especially when it attacks or undermines Judeo-
Christian beliefs. Robert Mapplethorpe's blatantly
anti-Christian and tax supported propaganda-art is a good
example. However, the Christian culture has made the fatal
flaw in defining itself only through negatives. We tell the
world we are against this and against that. But what are we
for? Where are the Christian artists, visionaries, filmmakers, television producers, etc.? Are we providing a true
creative alternative?

If indeed we are in the battle for the heart and mind of
mankind, then where are our artists and visionaries? The
reason that the contemporary Christian culture is desperately
lacking artists is because it has adopted the non-biblical idea

of being essentially anti-art and anti-creativity. As a consequence, creative people have left the Church in droves and have become the secular artists of our day.

Why is this important? In an article in *Charisma* magazine Charles Paul Conn, author and president of Lee College, writes these words: "After twenty years as a Christian father, youth minister and college professor, I have come to an emphatic conclusion: yes, this is a more dangerous day, spiritually, than any before. It is more difficult to bring our children into a saving knowledge of Christ. After many years of saying, 'it ain't so,' I am now convinced that it is a most hazardous period for our young people, and the threat of losing the next generation is greater than it has ever been in the past." He goes on to add, "The technology of the 1990s, which has offered us a path into world evangelism, has also opened a channel for Satan into our homes. The day of air-tight, sin-proof, hermetically sealed Christian home in which the purity of the children depends on the vigilance of the father, is gone forever. The blend of overprotection and legalism that kept sin from the door of a generation ago is no longer effective."[4]

The means of mass communication are in competition with Christian values. If those who reject God in favor of New Age beliefs present their beliefs more effectively and creatively than Christians do, then we are going to lose the battle for the heart and mind of mankind!

What is needed is a reformation in the Christian culture in regard to creativity and art under the Lordship of Jesus Christ and the raising up of a new generation of Christian artists and visionaries. This will not happen in a vacuum however, it will only happen as Christian leaders and parents encourage and promote Christians in the arts and media. We must be willing to support such efforts with money, access to the religious media, and education.

The Great Deception

I remember going to the Bodhi Tree Bookstore which is the famous New Age bookstore on Melrose Avenue popularized in Shirley Maclaine's television movie "Out On A Limb." I rented a video that dealt with the "Higher Consciousness Movement." The topic was world peace.

The video featured people like Baba Ram Dass, who was formerly Dr. Richard Alpert—Timothy Leary's assistant at Harvard; Barbara Marx Hubbard; Ken Keyes, Jr., who is the author of *The Handbook To Higher Consciousness* and *The Hundredth Monkey;* and Daniel Ellsberg, the peace activist whom former president Richard Nixon investigated during Watergate.

As I listened to these people talk, I couldn't help but hear their sincerity and passion for world peace—a passion that we all share. Yet, as they talked about developing a planetary consciousness and an end to nuclear weapons, I noted a fervency that religion engenders. I didn't particularly have a problem with that; I could appreciate their zeal for creating a world of understanding and harmony. But, the more I listened to them, the more it dawned upon me that these people had turned the corner somewhere in their thinking. They were attempting to build a kind of heaven on earth—without God.

Something haunted me in their words, and I believe it was the fact that they were attempting to build peace without the Prince of Peace and create love without the true source of love, which is the personal, living God of the universe. These peace activists talked of a planetary consciousness. They spoke of becoming one with the universe. This sounds legitimate until you stop to think that these efforts at building one world and global peace without God are somehow quite empty and shallow.

This was difficult to comprehend because these people

were so kind and compassionate. On the human level they displayed a remarkable integrity.

> Beloved do not believe every spirit, but test the spirits to see whether they are from God; because many false prophets have gone out into the world. By this you know the Spirit of God: every spirit that confesses that Jesus Christ has come in the flesh is from God; and every spirit that does not confess Jesus is not from God; and that is the spirit of the anti-Christ, of which you have heard that it is coming, and now it is already in the world. (1 John 4:1-3, NAS)

It is a difficult thing to grasp this concept. But, if we take what the Bible says seriously, then we must come to understand that there is a conflict between God and Satan happening right here on earth. If there is salvation in no one else besides Christ, then a real problem emerges when we discuss the teachings of the various gurus, human potential and higher consciousness movements, Eastern religions, meditation, planetary consciousness, and so on. In fact, things like Scientology, Est, Lifespring, and the whole gamut of pseudo-spiritual empowerment programs take on a new perspective.

It is not that these programs and religions cannot offer limited benefits and assist in the release of human potential. It is a real mistake to paint such things in either black or white. In addition, I have seen people who have emerged from these human potential movements with a real release of creativity and power in their lives. The danger is that ultimately the leaders of these groups become substitute Messiahs. Their teaching begins to depart from the Bible often producing bondage and slavery to incorrect doctrines. Finally, these movements can take on a real spirit of the Antichrist in that they are offering a kind of personal and planetary salvation apart from Jesus Christ.

Most of these groups offer some limited degree of good.

But then they become counterfeit Gospels that lead people astray. Also, when these principles of "higher consciousness" or "enlightenment" teach that it is possible to build a kind of paradise on earth without Christ, they become dangerous and reminiscent of the serpent who promised Eve in the Garden that "they would be as gods."

The Antichrist of Revelation

It is very difficult to talk about the Antichrist as revealed in the Book of Revelation. There have been too many horror and science fiction books and films from *Omen* to *Exorcist III* that have dealt with the subject of 666 and the beast. To compound matters, late night cable television is replete with authors talking about the end of the world and offering their latest book or tape of prophecy.

If one is not careful, one can be hardened and calloused to all the showmanship surrounding what the Bible calls the Antichrist and miss the important warnings in the Scriptures. In Revelation the Apostle John writes:

> And I beheld another beast coming up out of the earth; and he had two horns like a lamb, and he spake as a dragon.

> And he exerciseth all the power of the first beast before him, and causeth the earth and them which dwell therein to worship the first beast, whose deadly wound was healed.

> And he doeth great wonders, so that he maketh fire come down from heaven on the earth in the sight of men.

> And deceiveth them that dwell on the earth by the means of those miracles which he had power to do in the sight of the beast; saying to them of the world to make a great statue of the first Creature, who was fatally wounded and then came back to life. He was permitted to give

breath to this statue and even make it speak! Then
the statue ordered that anyone refusing to
worship it must die!

He required everyone—great and small, rich and
poor, slave and free—to be tattooed with a certain mark on the right hand or on the forehead.
And no one could get a job or even buy in any
store without the permit of that mark, which was
either the name of the Creature or the code
number of his name. Here is a puzzle that calls
for careful thought to solve it. Let those who are
able, interpret this code: the numerical values of
the letters in his name add to 666! (Rev. 13:11-
18, AV)

In these passages of Scripture the Bible warns of a
charismatic world leader who will emerge. He will rule the
world and create a new economic system where people
cannot buy or sell without the mark of the "beast," which is
666. At first glance all this sounds like something from a
Clive Barker or Stephen King novel. It sounds too fantastic
to be true.

However, we must understand that the spirit of the
Antichrist is already in the world. The spirit of this age
attempts to find personal and planetary paradise apart from
God. It is the same spirit that causes men to place self above
all else. In addition, powerful socioeconomic forces are
aligning to create a one world government and monetary
system that will one day invite a super authoritarian leader
to take control.

However, the Bible is not clear as to exactly when this
will occur. Despite the fact that there are currently many
prophesies being fulfilled with regard to Christ's return, we
do mankind a great disservice by making wild predictions
and assumptions based on specious arguments. The net
effect of all this drum beating is that many have become like

the boy who falsely cried wolf so many times that when there really was danger nobody listened.

Powerful social, economic, political, and religious forces are shaping our world; we know that at some point in the future prophecy will be fulfilled regarding both the Second Coming and the Antichrist. But, poor exegesis and conjecture can blind us to the many opportunities that are available for evangelism.

Blind fatalism is very dangerous and can be a cop out for not being involved with the problems of society and humanity. It's easy to ignore AIDS, poverty, the destruction of society, real needs for evangelism, and the plight of suffering people when we are glued to our television sets waiting for the rapture.

All of the Bible's prophecies will come true; becoming intelligent and informed about them is important. However, the purpose of prophecy is not to stir fear and endless speculation about supposed end time events. The purpose of prophecy is to build a passion for reaching people for Jesus Christ and changing our world. Commenting on this, the General Secretary of the Baptist Union of Great Britain and Ireland, D.S. Russell asserts that

> Christians have identified their persecutors and oppressors as the Antichrist whose appearance is to succeed the Second Advent. In this way a long line of tyrants from Nero to Hitler has been recognized and Christians have seen in the persecution of the faithful at their hands sure sign that the end is near.

> Identification of the Antichrist has occupied the time of cranks and credulous alike. And yet the notion itself is not to be dismissed with a superior sniff, for surely the Antichrist, whether he be called by that name or not, represents a reality against which all Christians must be on their guard. That reality is the presence in our universe

of what Paul describes as "principalities and powers" whose evil influence is to be found not just in evil men but also institutions, nations and states which share man's falleness and also his delusion that they too can be as God.

A War in Heaven

"And there was a war in heaven, Michael and his angels waging war with the dragon. And the dragon and his angels waged war" (Rev. 12:7).

The book of Revelation clearly indicates that there was an actual war going on in heaven between the dragon who is Satan and Michael and his angels who are on God's side. In verses eight through nine of Revelation chapter 12 John says, "and they were not strong enough, and there was no longer a place found for them in heaven. And the great dragon was thrown down, the serpent of old who is called the devil and Satan, who deceives the whole world, he was thrown down to earth, and his angels were thrown down with him."

In these passages of Scripture we see that the war in heaven between God and Satan is now continued on earth. Right now there is a war going on in the invisible realm and in the physical realm between the demons and the angels and God and the devil. However, for most people the automatic response to reading about this war is total denial. The information is too heavy. It literally overloads the human computer. Therefore, the secularists and mystics of our age dismiss the thought of an actual war between good and evil as allegorical or mythological. Yet, God's Word states that there is a war between God and the devil. It is occurring at this moment.

We must understand that there is a spiritual element to all human affairs and history and that the historical flow of events is not merely circumstantial but spiritual. For example, the rise to power of Adolf Hitler was not just the product of human engineering and manipulation. In the invisible realm there were powers of darkness that energized Adolf Hitler and who had a systematic hatred of God's chosen people, the Jews. Behind the scenes, the establishment of the Third Reich was spiritual. These powers of darkness in the invisible realm were allowed to take control because of the absence of light. God's people, both Christians and Jews, were apathetic and they did not intercede or stand up for what was right. The consequence was that evil was allowed to gain control of a society.

It has been said that "the price of freedom is eternal vigilance." We have seen in Revelation 12:7-9 that the devil has been thrown down to the earth. Evil is always waiting for an opportunity to move forward and bring death and destruction. This is the very nature of the Beast. Evil must advance like a cancer until it is stopped or cut out. True good can never coexist with pure evil. One or the other will triumph in the end.

In Ephesians 6:12 the Apostle Paul states: "For our struggle is not against flesh and blood, but against the rulers, against the powers, against the world forces of this darkness, against the spiritual forces of wickedness in the heavenly places." Every human problem whether political, physical, psychological, or relational has a spiritual dimension. The reason modern political or psychological theory is so ineffective is because it fails to deal adequately with the true nature and existence of the invisible realm.

For example, sexual problems such as homosexuality, child abuse, and sexual perversions do have a spiritual element. There can be a spirit behind homosexuality, child abuse, and perversion that literally grips people and captures their minds and spirits. True freedom can sometimes only be found in a supernatural act of deliverance and through a distinct severing of the powers of darkness by the authority of Jesus Christ. There are cases when demonic oppression must be broken in the invisible realm.

The same is true for alcoholism and drug addiction.

Often the addiction is more than chemical or psychological. Organizations like Alcoholics Anonymous understand this. There can be a need for a breaking of the spirit of addiction or the spirit behind alcoholism or drug addiction. This is why an organization like Teen Challenge, founded by Rev. David Wilkerson in New York City, was so effective in curing heroin addicts while governmental agencies failed. Rev. Wilkerson and his staff ministered supernatural deliverance by the power of the Holy Spirit to the addicts.

On the political level we see the influence of principalities and powers in the invisible realm. In fact, over every geographic location, town, city, and nation there are principalities and powers in the invisible realm. They are attempting to exercise dominion, and unless they are bound by an interceding church, they will maintain their control.

The Proper Confrontation

William Shakespeare penned the immortal lines "All the world's a stage, and all the men and women merely players." Those words are true, especially in relation to the nature of warfare in multi-dimensions. We should look at life as a play in which there are two competing playwrights, the personal God and Lucifer, competing for the heart and mind of mankind. Each of us are actors in one play or the other. If we could see this play from a million miles above the earth, we would come to a rude awakening. Especially those with Judeo-Christian moral beliefs and perspectives.

The play written by God and the actors in it will ultimately triumph. In this act, however, we are being tricked by the playwright from the opposing side. We are playing the part of a cultural enemy and thus enemies to all of life. We have been seduced by the serpent of old into standing on the outside of the culture, bitterly complaining about it and throwing stones from over a giant wall of pietism. It's as if this brilliant evil playwright has tricked the actors in the most brilliant play ever written by God to stop reading their lines written by God and read the enemy's lines while the audience laughs and jeers.

We were never supposed to become the enemies of culture and life. And yet, in the great cultural battle, there are those who claim a Judeo-Christian world view who have defined this view by standing on the outside of culture, e.g., movies, art, politics, education, science and philosophy, and ridiculing it. This does absolutely nothing but force people to reject all that is good and holy in the universe. This is not to say that we should not stand up for what is right—we should. But our victory can only be found by rising up in a great and glorious anthem to the Son. We must be torch bearers of a better world and a future kingdom. We must march in infinite creativity to recapture the cultural flag as it were. Not through censorship, but through presenting a burning and magnificent vision of Paradise restored and splitting contemporary reality in two with the awesome thunderous magnificence of a God who really is there! In symphony, with these purposes the secular walls of Jericho, the fortresses of humanism, materialism, and sexual anarchy will crash and burn before the magnificent array of an earthly army infused with the glory of a heavenly light.

Chapter Four

Millennium III

What is the future of America and the world going to hold? Are we heading toward Armageddon, nuclear destruction, and ecological disaster, or are we going to build Paradise on earth? Mankind is racing toward a destiny as yet unknown. However, will it be peace and prosperity or global totalitarianism with unequaled oppression and bloodshed?

Unlike many of the so-called prophets of doom, the rosy eyed optimists predict a new Utopia. I do not believe the future is fixed. It is true, God does know the future. However, we have been given the power of free will and choice. We will determine our collective destiny. The prophetic book of Revelation will unfold exactly as God predicted it would. But it will be a future radically different than what the vast majority of so-called prophets have outlined.

Mankind is on the brink of a brand new world and the emergence of a New World Order. The human race is entering an era of untold magnificence and technological breakthrough as well as a series of sudden disasters and holocausts.

However, just like our real space-time-genetic ancestors were given the power of free choice in the Garden of Eden, so today the human race has been given an empty canvas on which to paint its destiny. If we were to walk through a museum of paintings that depict the history of mankind, we would see an entire spectrum of human events. As we walked through these galleries of space and time, we would see the beauty of a sunset, romantic lovers walking on a beach, Leonardo da Vinci's *Madonna* as well as wars I, II and possibly III. For the human race is capable of the divine and the hellish, and our history is a composition of both.

Our future will be composed of unparalleled greatness and the hideous monstrosities represented by such things as the millions murdered under Joseph Stalin and Adolf Hitler or those killed during the Beijing Massacre.

Although God is the Supreme Being and we are in a titanic struggle with the forces of evil, mankind has been given the power of free will and choice. Since our future is yet unwritten, it is up to us in relationship with the personal, living God of the universe to turn back the forces of evil and establish the reign of love on planet Earth.

The Shape of Things to Come

America and the rest of the world is racing to the future. What's on the horizon? Things like geodesic dome houses, robot butlers, kill pills, electronic psychedelic drugs, video telephones, three dimensional television, simulated African safaris, and a host of new inventions.

The capacity for good and evil will be increased in the near future. Many churches will televise their Bible studies and Sunday services through cable television in an unprecedented manner. Even small churches will be able to keep in contact with their congregation electronically. The pornography industry will get into three dimensional television rather quickly and will offer electronic simulated fantasy sex where people will electronically enter their sexual fantasies.

The average American is totally unprepared for what technology is about to unleash on us—good and bad. Underground pornographers using new electronics and three dimensional television will offer deviant recreated sexual fantasies. Interactive sadomasochism, rape, violent sexuality, ritual satanic killings, and child abuse will be bootlegged into people's homes through computers and videos. Already a market exists for computerized Nintendo-like sex games.

The world is quickly becoming like science fiction writer William Gibson's vision of the future—a world of alternate human realities inside computer games, which he describes in his book *Neuromancer*.

Some New Age organizations network electronically around the globe via computers. In fact, riding in a cab to the Virginia Beach airport (after hosting the Christian Broadcasting Network's National Conference on the New Age Movement), a lady whose husband was connected to the military told me about a secret group called the First Earth Battalion. This was a former New Age think tank and strike force that existed inside the army. They were linked up by computer across the United States. This woman had a computer in her home that was linked into this system of people who communicate across the country—until the government disbanded it.

Technology is going to completely alter the face of life on our planet. We can expect an initiative to change state, local, and national elections with computers. Instead of going to a polling place, each citizen (linked up with millions of other citizens through the phone lines) will be able to watch an issue or candidate presented on television and vote immediately. The election will be decided in minutes. Entire cities such as Los Angeles and New York City will be able to vote on homeless bills, AIDS legislation and other bills weekly. Computers will rapidly transform our political process. There may be hidden powers who will try to prevent the spread of this democratization process. Those segments of the populace who are informed on the issues and active either Left or Right will run the various cities and the nation.

Imagine an issue such as the controversial National Endowment of the Arts funding of the Robert Mapplethorpe exhibit. This featured close ups of children's genitalia and homosexual acts. What would happen if the population of the United States could be polled nightly regarding this or other issues?

Scientists and Visionaries Who Are Designing the Future

The cultural leadership of our society is primarily in the hands of those who hold a materialist or Eastern mystical world view of the universe. The future is being designed by modern thinkers and social engineers who do not acknowledge the existence of a personal, living God. Nor do they share in the idea that man is the unique creation of this God. They admit no difference in kind between human and infra human, yet they fail to explain man's rational powers of conceptual thought. Our ability to abstract the moral law or draw any prescriptive conclusions is most befuddling to these modern thinkers. "All men by nature," says Aristotle in his *Ethics*, "desire to know." We are indeed unique among all creatures of the earth. We are created in God's image. There is a part of us that is not reducible to atoms or subatomic particles. This cannot be said of any other thing on earth. Only man has a spirit!

These social engineers attempt to build a brave new world by tinkering with powerful forces that, although Utopian in outlook, will produce the dehumanization and enslavement of the human race.

For example, psychologist B.F. Skinner's utopian novel, *Walden II,* presents a future community built on Skinner's ideas of behavior modification and conditioning techniques. Futurists and social engineers have used Skinner's "behavior mod" techniques in attempting to restructure society.

Both *The Humanist Manifesto I* and *The Humanist Manifesto II* have brought us closer to what George Orwell wrote about in his novel *1984* where the Ministry of Truth used slogans such as "War is Peace," "Freedom is Slavery," "Ignorance is Truth." We have such double talk slogans in our culture when we say "Pro-Choice" but mean the right to murder babies or "If It Feels Good Do It" when we mean giving in to our most base instincts and so on.

Social Engineers of a Brave New World

Scientific data, statistics, and research play an important role in changing the way society behaves and what it thinks about itself. By manipulating and creating data that supports a particular political or social philosophy and promoting this data, many scientists have promoted their agenda. Attempts are made by modern social engineers to create a new kind of society based on their particular beliefs whether they are valid or not.

For example, in the book *Kinsey, Sex and Fraud* authors Dr. Judith A. Reisman and Edward W. Eichel allege that the supposed scientific research on human

sexuality conducted by Alfred C. Kinsey in the Kinsey
Report was fraudulent.[1] In fact, world famous psychologist
Abraham Maslow challenged Kinsey's use of volunteers
as a reliable means of getting data. Also, Reisman and
Eichel assert that Kinsey used sex offenders and prisoners
to get much of his data and that they were not representative
of the population as a whole.

In fact, Dr. Judith A. Reisman believes that Alfred C.
Kinsey had a specific hidden agenda to create a sexual
revolution and purposely loaded his data to support that
result. According to Dr. J. Gordon Muir and Edward W.
Eichel, Kinsey reached the three following conclusions:

1. The normal expression of human sexuality is
bisexuality. That this capacity is not realized in many
people is because of "cultural restraints" and societal
inhibitions, which are assumed to be negative influen-
ces.

2. Sexual contact with adults would be a normal part
of growing up with children in a less inhibited society.

3. Promiscuity and diversity of sexual expression cor-
relate with sexual health (*Kinsey, Sex and Fraud* pg.
215).

Kinsey's faulty research was used by social activists,
the mass media, educators, and the pornography industry
as the basis for creating a sexual revolution. Hugh Hefner
of *Playboy* magazine credits Kinsey for many of his beliefs,
and *Playboy* has funded organizations like the Masters and
Johnson Institute as well as the initial grant to establish the
Office of Research Services of the Sex Information Council and Education Council of the U.S. (SIECUS).

In addition, educators across the country have
promoted Kinsey's ideas in sex education courses that have
literally indoctrinated students with radical ideas on
promiscuity, homosexuality, and abortion, all based on

research that was manufactured to create a sexual revolution.

Over and over again in our society we see forms of social engineering being undertaken that are not any less significant than Chairman Mao's restructuring of China. It is being initiated by those who have hidden social agendas that are deliberately obscured by powerful interest groups. For example, important facts about Planned Parenthood's founder Margaret Sanger who wrote about her desire to breed a race of supermen and women through the sterilization of "black people," "Jews," and "mentally defective" is hidden by the media from the American public. The fact that Margaret Sanger believed in the Hitlerian idea of eugenics totally undermines Planned Parenthood as a credible organization. Also, the fact that Roger Baldwin, founder of the ACLU, declared at Harvard in 1935 that he wanted to create a "workers' state" in the U.S. and that the ACLU was established to defend "Bolsheviks" are important facts that are hidden from most Americans. It seems when it comes to things like scientific proof that disproves Darwinian evolution, the unreliability of the Kinsey reports, the eugenics philosophy behind the creation of Planned Parenthood, the Communist beliefs of the ACLU's founder, Roger Baldwin, and on and on, facts and research are allowed to be manipulated to create a mythology that promotes a New World Order. This is nothing less than what George Orwell wrote about in his novel *1984*.

Isaac Asimov and the Humanist Perspective

Isaac Asimov is the author of books on science, chemistry, astronomy, physics, biology, children's books, history, the Bible, and his famous science fiction books including the *Foundation* series. Asimov is president of the

American Humanist Association and is an activist for promoting the humanistic philosophy.

In an interview with broadcaster Bill Moyers reprinted in the *Humanist* magazine (Jan.-Feb. 1989) Asimov intelligently explains the humanist position regarding religion. Bill Moyers asked Asimov the question, "Are you the enemy of religion?" Asimov responded, "No, I'm not as it seems any civilized, humane person should feel, that every person has the right to his own beliefs and his own securities and his own likings. What I'm against is attempting to place a person's belief system onto the nation or the world generally. . . . And my objection to fundamentalism is not that they are fundamentalists but that they essentially want me to be a fundamentalist too. . . . Now they say they want to teach creationism on an equal basis. But they can't; it's not a science."

Here we see in Bill Moyers' interview several interesting things. First, Isaac Asimov truly believes that he is objective, compassionate, and interested in truth at all costs. In many ways, he is the ideal humanist because he believes in a diversity of opinion. However, Asimov, like many humanists and some in the biblical world view camp, has a blind side. He is absolutely convinced, for example, that there is no scientific evidence for creationism. He is certain that the Bible is incompatible with science. This is a false premise and reflects a genuine misunderstanding of what Christianity is all about. If the Bible is truth, then it must be historic, scientific, and sociological truth as well as religious truth. Part of the reason for the general misunderstanding regarding the Scriptures is that many people ascribe to the Bible what it does not say. For example, the Bible does not say there were no dinosaurs and concerning the earth's age and mankind's age the Bible does not disagree with science.

In addition, much is revealed by the tone of Bill Moyer's questions when he comments, ". . . this is what frightens, many, many believers. They see science as uncertain, always tentative, always subject to revisionism. They see science as a complex, chilling and enormous universe, ruled by chance and impersonal laws. They see science as dangerous."

An interesting thing is revealed in these comments and they are not entirely untrue. There are large segments of those who call themselves believers who fit into this category. They believe in Christ apart from reason. They erroneously think that science and the Bible are incompatible. In fact, I know Christians who are scientists and psychologists who practice a form of spiritual schizophrenia in that they believe in the Bible when it comes to "spiritual" things but not when it comes to scientific or historical matters. This is the classic liberal theological position. Yet, it is ridiculous because it undermines the very intelligence and authority of God. We do not believe the Bible because we are cringing fundamentalists hiding out in the corners of society desperately praying that we will not be found out. This is absurd, the God of history and the reliability of the Bible have never contradicted scientific evidence when that evidence has been proven. It is when science enters the arena of conjecture and half-truths that science conflicts with the Bible. For example, Darwin had some correct ideas. But, when applied to the origin of the human species they are unproven. Science takes a "leap of faith" in order to accept them apart from evidence. It is when science becomes religion that the two clash and that is what has often happened in our day.

Finally Moyers asked Asimov the question, "Do you see any room for reconciling the two world views: the religious, the biblical view, the universe as God's drama, constantly interrupted and rewritten by divine intervention and the universe as scientists hold it . . ." Asimov answers by concluding that religion and science cannot mix unless there is scientific evidence for God's existence.

Yet, there has been scientific evidence for God's existence. The accuracy of Old Testament prophecies coming true concerning Christ, the archeological findings and evidence of Christ's resurrection echoes across history; the "five ways" in which, according to Aquinas, the existence of God can be proved *a posteriori* (the best known being Aristotle's argument from motion). Not to mention the millions of lives dynamically transformed by those who have encountered the living God.

No matter how sincere Asimov might be, ultimately he is blinded by his faith and prejudice in humanism, which is the very thing he accuses believers in God of being. In short, his belief has not been demonstrated to be true by the empirical methods of science. He holds on to his belief in spite of reason, not because of it!

Important Future Trends

Man has attempted to predict the future since before Plato wrote his *Republic*. Men like Sir Thomas Moore wrote *Utopia*, Sir Francis Bacon wrote *New Atlantis*, Hans Christian Andersen wrote about young Americans who would cross the Atlantic in steam driven flying machines, and Jules Verne wrote *From Earth to Moon* before the advent of space travel.

Then in the twentieth century men like H.G. Wells attempted to predict the future with books like *The Time Machine* and *When The Sleeper Awakes*. H.G. Wells accurately foresaw the decline of horse-drawn vehicles, the coming of motor trucks, and the importance of aviation in warfare. More recently authors like Arthur C. Clarke, who wrote *2001: A Space Odyssey* and *2100* along with Issac Asimov, who wrote the *Foundation Trilogy* have attempted to walk in the footsteps of Verne and Wells.

Although predicting the future is not an accurate science, we can examine current trends and make reasonable predictions regarding future trends. The following is a list of trends regarding our future that I believe will seriously affect us. This information was compiled from exhaustive reading and magazines like the *Futurist, Think Tanks* by Paul Dixon and *The Study of The Future—An Introduction to the Art and Science of Understanding* and *Shaping Tomorrow's World* by Edward Cornish with members of the World Future Society. Here are some of the trends.

* Computers will replace drugs as a means of getting people high. Computers originally developed for training pilots in simulated flight conditions will create a condition called virtual reality. This takes the user into cyberspace.   The result is a powerful psychedelic experience as powerful as any drug without physical addictions. We can expect young people and drug users to buy small computers that will give them highs far more powerful than LSD and cocaine.

* Despite the current recession U.S. society will grow to remarkable levels of affluence possibly tripling the GNP from present levels in the near future.

* Traditional world cities such as New York, Tokyo, London, and Los Angeles will become giant megalopolises that will stretch for hundreds of miles. An example is Southern California, which is quickly becoming one super city that stretches from San Diego to Santa Barbara.

* Unfortunately, cars will still be around and will

continue to create massive traffic jams. The helicopter cars portrayed in the movie the *Jetsons* will not be a practical reality. Gasoline may be substituted by another fuel.

* There will be 6 billion people on planet Earth by the time we reach the year a.d. 2000 and 10 billion by 2050 if the Lord tarries. This growth will not be strong in Europe or America. It will primarily occur in Third World nations. Clearly, evangelism will be centered in those nations.

* It is a matter of time until nuclear weapons are used again. They will be far more devastating than the atomic bombs dropped on Hiroshima and Nagasaki. It is probable that these weapons will be used by a renegade nation like Iraq and not a super power like the United States or the U.S.S.R. However, a first strike by a nation like Iraq using nuclear weapons would precipitate a nuclear counter attack by a super power such as the United States or Israel.

* The United States will continue to decline as a world power while United Europe grows stronger. Excessive federal regulations and a growing governmental bureaucracy will inhibit the United States from reaching its full potential.

* Although the name New Age will become passe just as the word hippie did, Eastern mystical and occult religions will continue to win millions of converts including the elite of our nation.

* Due to the apathy of those calling themselves Christians, laws and public policies restricting the freedom of religion will continue.

* Now with the advent of NC-17, X-rated films under the guise of art will proliferate with mainstream filmmakers using explicit sexual acts in mainstream

films that will be rated NC-17. In addition, television soap operas and movies will feature explicit sex scenes during prime time.

* There are now reported 12 millions cases of sexually transmitted diseases per year. Sexually transmitted diseases such as AIDS, herpes, and chlamydia will escalate to unprecedented numbers. The AIDS epidemic alone will force a crisis in the health insurance industry.

* According to UNICEF statistics, forty thousand children die each day from hunger and hunger related diseases. As economies crumble and populations increase, that number could easily triple to 120,000 children daily succumbing to hunger.

* Since abortion was legalized in 1973, twenty-five to thirty million babies have been killed. Currently, 1.5 million babies are aborted each year. With the introduction of the French abortion pill RU-486 this figure could climb again.

* In the last election only 33 percent of the eligible voters actually voted. This number should continue to go down as voter apathy increases due to a heavily entrenched bureaucracy.

* Children from the ages of six to eighteen watch an average of sixteen thousand hours of television. Conversely, they spend only twelve thousand hours in school. The typical teenager will have seen 150,000 violent episodes on television and twenty-five thousand killings by the time he or she graduates. AS NC-17 movies and cable television expands, we can expect this figure to continue to grow.

If statistics and trends are like thermometers in the mouth of a sick patient, then our nation is clearly on a downward spiral. The reason things are getting worse is because the society as a whole is operating from a humanistic viewpoint. The guiding philosophy by which our world operates is faulty and as such the decisions and choices we make are leading us down a wrong path. One could easily throw up one's hands in despair and declare that it is of no use or run around like the proverbial "chicken little" shouting "the sky is falling . . . the sky is falling." However, although society appears to be getting worse and out of control, an intelligent minority with a plan built on biblical perspectives can change the course of human history. This does not mean that we can reverse prophetic trends nor should we. Yet, the Bible never called us to fatalism and despair. Every person who believes in God and goodness must become active not in the fanatical or extreme sense, but in the sense of praying, standing in the gap, and seeking the Lord where we might make a difference!

The Abortion Pill—RU-486

Pro-choice groups are lobbying to import an abortion pill called RU-486 from a French manufacturer, Roussel Uclaf. The drug was first developed in France in 1988 and is a synthetic steroid that induces an abortion by blocking the effect of progesterone, a hormone needed in a successful pregnancy. In addition, RU-486 is thought to be beneficial in blocking cancerous breast tumors. Pro-life groups have charged that the supposed medical benefits of RU-486 are attempts to disguise the fact that the French pill is in reality a "death drug."

It is likely, that RU-486 or a similar drug will become available soon in the United States either legally or illegally. When that time comes pregnant teenage and adult women will be able to pop a tiny pill and "kill" their babies in the privacy of their home. In fact, they will literally be able to flush them down the toilet.

The Right to Die—Euthanasia

The flip side of the abortion movement is the Right To Die movement. As the graying of America continues and the baby boomer generation along with their parents grow older, euthanasia or the right to die will become a major issue.

Derek Humphry, age sixty, is the founder of the National Hemlock Society, which promotes "the right to die" for terminally ill patients and the so-called death with dignity. Once again, if you accept a materialist world view and you really believe there is no reason for living and no life after death, then euthanasia makes sense. However, if you believe that you are here for a purpose and that you will be judged for your life and that there is a Creator, then euthanasia becomes a crime against the divine order and life itself.

Humphry's organization is growing rapidly with a newsletter that goes out to thirty-six thousand members in sixty-seven chapters around the country. Media attention has been focused on the "right to die" because Janet Adkins, a National Hemlock member, took her life with the help of a suicide machine invented by a Detroit doctor, Jack Kevorian.

Derek Humphry is mobilizing to create legislation that would make euthanasia, or "self-deliverance" as he calls it, become legal as it did in Holland where the courts sanctioned it in 1984. In California Humphry tried to get a "right to die" ballot measure passed, but failed.

Humphry assisted his wife in a suicide with a poisoned cup of coffee filled with pain killers and sleeping pills because she was suffering from bone cancer. Since then he has been on a crusade for euthanasia.

In fact, the time could come when your local drug store

chain will not only carry the abortion pill RU-486 but also Dr. Kevorian's suicide machine. If it sounds like a "Brave New World," it's because it is.

Persecution against Christians in America

For those who say it can't happen here—it is already happening here in America. Christians are being increasingly persecuted for their beliefs and bold stand for Jesus Christ. The FBI has issued a warning to churches across the country to be on the look out for bombs in the mail. According to Jamie Buckingham, Postal Inspector C.W. Lawrence has issued a special bulletin to churches entitled "Bombs By Mail" in order to warn churches of the growing threat.

Rev. John Osteen, pastor of the Lakewood Church in Houston, has already experienced one such attack. Rev. Osteen's daughter opened a "bomb by mail" that exploded and threw shrapnel across the room. Miraculously she was relatively unharmed by the explosion, which should have killed her. In addition, a pipe bomb in the mail targeted for Pat Robertson exploded in the CBN mail room in Virginia Beach, Virginia harming no one.

Gospel singer Sandi Patti had her offices burned down on 17 April 1990 by a group called the Equal Religious Coalition with damages placed at $650,000. Local newspaper and radio stations received statements from the Equal Religious Coalition that accused Patti of "blatancy to put herself on the pedestal of God."

Dr. Larry Poland, who formed Master Media as an outreach to executives in the entertainment industry and who was instrumental in organizing the protest against the *Last Temptation of Christ,* warns of a growing attack against Christians in America in his book *The Coming Persecution.* Poland believes that American Christians are going to experience increased persecution in the days ahead.

Recently, American Portrait Films has produced a movie entitled *The Brutal Truth*. This powerful documentary shows actual footage of police brutality against Operation Rescue demonstrators. In the footage, policemen use the martial arts weapon called a "numb chuck." They broke the bones of one demonstrator on camera. The level of police brutality against Operation Rescue was so intense that if it had been any other group, there would have been a media outcry. Yet, because the media is pro-abortion, they remained silent in the face of such brutality. One can assume that the liberal media's interest in civil rights extends only to the civil rights of those they agree with philosophically. In reality, the whole episode exposes the myth of media neutrality once and for all.

Finally, American troops stationed in the Persian Gulf were not allowed to receive Bibles or religious literature from home. The U.S. government issued a policy stating that no Bibles or religious literature could be mailed to the soldiers. If the troops could not enjoy their Constitutional rights such as freedom of religion, one wonders exactly why they were over there fighting.

Anti-Christian Bigotry

Even the conservative *Wall Street Journal* joined the Christian bashing frenzy in a recent article by Robert Johnson who took on the entire Assembly of God denomination in a front page article entitled "Heavenly Gifts—Preaching a Gospel of Acquisitiveness, A Showy Sect Prospers" (11 Dec. 1990). What an outrage! The *Wall Street Journal* accuses the Assemblies of God with over

3,900,000 followers and 11,300 churches of being a "showy sect."

Then Rev. Tommy Barnett of the Phoenix First Assembly of God Church in Arizona is mocked and ridiculed with remarks like "this Pentecostal Peter Pan in a gray suit . . ." The mass media in our nation relentlessly attack anything that even remotely champions morality or Judeo-Christian values.

The reason the media continues to assault the Church is because many in church confuse passivity with spirituality due to the acceptance of the non-biblical theology of pietism, which asserts that it is spiritual to be removed from moral conflict. It is precisely because of this theological position that biblical Christianity is being pushed into the basement of our society by secular bullies. These bullies will continue to beat up on their opponents until they stand up and fight for their rights!

This whole concept of non-involvement in politics and moral issues by Christians in society is a form of psuedo-spirituality that prevents a biblical and active participation in our c ulture. This is exactly the same mistake the evangelical church made in Germany prior to the takeover by Adolf Hitler. We must remember that the Nazis were able to take control of Germany and slaughter millions of Jews because of the passivity of the Church.

The Coming Dictatorship of America

The biggest myth ever to be invented is happening right here under our noses in America—the myth or lie that "It Can't Happen Here!" This is exactly what the Jews were saying while Adolf Hitler came to power and even when the Nazis began gassing the Jews in Auschwitz. Human beings have the amazing capacity to live in a state of psychological denial when something bad is going on.

Families demonstrate this when children are being sexually abused or often when alcoholism enters the picture. Many in our culture and specifically Christians are in a state of denial about what is happening in our nation.

Just look at what's happening on television. Pro-life demonstrators are being thrown in jail and violently assaulted by the police while the secular media blacks it out. Christians are being arrested for holding Bible studies in their homes, churches are being shut down for having Sunday school classes and not registering them with the government. America is sliding toward a totalitarian state. However, unlike in Nazi Germany, it is happening very subtly. At the present moment, America has not yet experienced an economic collapse and SS Troops are not rampaging people's homes. A more insidious plot has developed. An ever growing federal bureaucracy is forcing its way into our lives.

If Christians remain silent, it won't be long until local police departments in middle class neighborhoods will issue citations for having home prayer meetings. References to Christ and the Christian religion (already removed from the classroom) will be stripped from all public and political institutions. There are forces at work in our society today that are trying to remove "In God We Trust" from our monetary currency; and in the name of "freedom" they are persecuting the Church.

Unless we have a national revival and reformation, we are not far away from the time when it will be illegal to publicly practice our Christianity.

Christians must respond to God's call to be the "salt of the earth" and influence the society in which we are members.

High Noon

Western civilization, America, and the free world is at high noon. Like the great western with Cary Grant, the outlaws have gotten off the train and are heading to town. Unless we fight these ideological outlaws intelligently and decisively, we, as Jews and Christians who embrace the Judeo-Christian perspective, will be gunned down in the public square.

It is a moral outrage in our nation that candidates for public office would mount offensively pro-abortion platforms. John Van DeKamp in California openly came out in favor of the French "kill pill," an abortion inducing chemical. Where are the millions of people who embrace family values in the state of California? Why is there not a storm of protest? The Bible warns, "woe unto them who sit idly by while the innocent are slain." If we do not speak up, soon there will be no one left to speak up.

Can we not hear the marching boots of oppression in the distance? Are we deaf to the crescendo of voices in our country that are crying out for the abolition of religion and the family—the repeal of our Constitutional freedoms?

> In Germany they came first for the Communists, and then I didn't speak up because I wasn't a Communist. Then they came for the Jews, and I didn't speak up because I wasn't a Jew. Then they came for the trade unionists, and I didn't speak up because I wasn't a trade unionist. Then they came for the Catholics, and I didn't speak up because I was a Protestant. Then they came for me, and by that time no one was left to speak up. (Martin Niemoller)

The Campaign to Create Public Hatred for Christians and Jews

Before Adolf Hitler was able to slaughter millions of

Jews in the gas chambers or death camps such as Aus-
witchz, he first had to embark on a propaganda campaign
to create hatred for the Jews. In order for good middle class
Germans to join the Nazi party and to participate in the
holocaust, they first had to be brainwashed to develop a
fanatical hatred for the Jewish people. The Jews had to be
blamed for the problems of Germany. Only then would the
German people be willing to exterminate the Jewish people
and to keep silent while the holocaust happened. Today the
cry from Jewish activists is "Never Again!" and they have
developed a needed militant defense of the nation of Israel
and the Jewish religion and culture around the world.

However, in our nation a new and insidious form of
religious hatred is developing. I believe there is an attempt
to create hatred in the public mind toward orthodox Christians, Jews, and Catholics. It is being implemented by the
mass media. This is the first step in religious persecution.
If it is not stopped in its infancy, it will lead to an eventual
holocaust against Christians. A culture that will destroy its
unborn babies through abortion on the alters of sexual
pleasure and convenience, and a culture that considers
killing the elderly through euthanasia, is not far from
exterminating "undesirables" such as Christians, Jews, and
Muslims.

Last night my wife and I watched the hit television
show "The Simpsons." There was a scene where a Christian
preacher was urging the burning of books. Although there
exists a tiny minority of Christians who hold this view, the
idea that Christian ministers are fanatical book burners is
a lie that the writer of "The Simpsons" is actively promoting. No one would have dared to attack a Jewish rabbi or a
gay like that. Yet, there is a consistent and relentless attack
against Christians, ministers, and Christianity. Unlike the
Jews who have courageously and boldly declared, "Never

Again!" there is an apathy in much of the Church that might one day cost them their freedom, if not their lives. This is not an isolated incident. Christians are usually portrayed as hypocritical, insensitive, rude, and stupid on television.

Almost daily, mass media undermine traditional values in our culture. Just look at the way all Christians are called "fundamentalists" in the most sneering and derogatory tones. When the media uses the word "fundamentalists" or "born again" or "Christian right-wing fundamentalists" they use it with the same evil intent that racists use the word "nigger" or the way people use the word "queer" or any other slur word designed to promote hatred. The intent is to imply that Christians are dangerous lunatics, fanatics, and terrorists. It is not accidental that the media uses the word fundamentalist. It is deliberately designed to create hatred.

Notice the way the media such as the *Los Angeles Times* and television networks almost always call the pro-life movement the "Anti-Abortion Movement," and they call   pro-abortion movement "Pro-Choice." This is not accidental. The media is fully aware that the term "Pro-Choice" is positive while "Anti-Abortion" is negative. They have consciously chosen to name the pro-life movement with a negative name in order to orchestrate its effectiveness.

How often do you see a normal, healthy, and happy family going to church or praying on national television? The answer is *never!* unless it is a movie about a religious cult or a telefilm like "Fall From Grace" about Jim and Tammy Baker. Yet, over 60 percent of the American population claims to believe in God and prays regularly. Millions go to church each Sunday. Television is supposed to reflect the lives of its viewers. However, it does not. Television represents the anti-religious bias of a small but powerful number of media people who are out to control the thinking of the masses.

Look at the way the camera moves whenever it covers Christians and Christian events. Watch the close-up on the bozo, weirdo, or the fanatical. There may be a thousand well dressed, intelligent, and sharp looking people who believe in God there; but the camera will somehow inevitably and mysteriously end up on the weirdest looking person. The idea is to communicate the message that Christianity is a religion of lunatics! Am I suggesting that directors, cameramen, and editors do this deliberately? Yes, maybe not as part of a conspiracy but it reflects a cynical, prejudiced, and condescending attitude toward faith in God that is used by those in power for wrong purposes.

Anti-Christian Propaganda

In recent years there has been a flood of anti-Christian propaganda in the film industry. Movies like *The Handmaid's Tale*, director Oliver Stone's *Talk Radio*, and Costa Gravas's *Betrayed* all deal with themes that imply that Christianity is synonymous with right wing extremist and fascism and that Christians and white supremacists go hand in hand.

The industry's goal is to convince people that Christianity is a religion of white racists, fascists, and censors who are out to set up a right wing dictatorship in America. The idea is that they must be stopped at any cost before they take over. Unfortunately, in this battle for the heart and mind of mankind there have been a tiny number of Christians who play right into this.

Evangelism implies reaching out to all with the love of Christ. Instead of evangelism we too often have a white evangelical attempt at homogenizing America that is thoroughly anti-biblical. There are encouragingly thousands of wonderful exceptions such as Bishop Meare's church in Washington, D.C. and the lively praise and worship rallies in South Africa, which are attended by both black and white and which the American media totally ignore.

True biblical Christianity should be a "rainbow coalition" of all nationalities and races. A "rainbow coalition," not in the way the Rev. Jesse Jackson uses it, but a church which represents the entire spectrum of God's creation from all races and nationalities. What if the personal God sitting on the Great Throne of Judgement was black? Clearly, Christ did not have blonde hair and blue eyes, in fact he had dark features and was Jewish. Just suppose the God of the universe manifested Himself as black? It must be remembered that God is not a white man's God or any other single race's God. If we truly believe that all men and women are made in the image of God, then we must acknowledge that God is black, white, oriental, Hispanic, and so on because we are created in God's image.

Soviet Persecution of Jews

As a model of just how far a totalitarian society can go in terms of stripping even the most minute religious practices from its citizens, we look to the Soviet Union. Here is the classic example of how only a small minority (10 percent) in the Communist party can interfere with the most basic details of religious practices of its people.

In the U.S.S.R. the Jewish people were not allowed by the state to practice bras milah or the rite of circumcision except for medical reasons. It is interesting to note why a government would even want to interfere with an apparently harmless ceremony lasting only twenty-five minutes. Yet, it is clear that this draconian government, built on the principles of Marxism, would systematically attempt to censor even the most innocent religious ceremonies of its people.

There are thirty thousand Soviet Jews in the Los Angeles area. The one organization aiding Soviet Jews has assisted in the circumcision of three thousand Jews who have immigrated from the Soviet Union.

The case of Soviet Jews being denied their religious rights exemplifies how far a government hostile to religious liberty will go in denying the most basic human rights of their people. This should be a message of warning to all those who take their religious liberties for granted in the United States.

Chapter Five

Choosing the Future

America and many nations around the world are at the crossroads. They will either move toward continued freedom and religious liberty or chaos and totalitarianism. Here in America we will either continue to be a free nation from which the Gospel of Jesus Christ is openly communicated or we will move quickly into a secularist superstate governed by a hidden elite who are opposed to the Judeo Christian world view.

Right now, we are in very dangerous waters. If we continue on our present path unchecked, we will soon become a far different America than our founding fathers intended. Totalitarianism in America will probably not be the open totalitarianism of Mao, Joseph Stalin, or Adolf Hitler. Totalitarianism in America will mean a powerful elite that will run the country hiding behind the illusion of democracy. However, this will be a democracy where true Christianity is basically outlawed from public life.

The danger here in America is the apathy and passivity of the vast majority of middle class evangelical Christians. They believe the lie "it can't happen here" while in reality it *is* happening here. Look closely at the news footage of pro-life demonstrators being handcuffed and churches being prohibited from teaching Sunday school without a license from the state. We are a long way down the road towards totalitarianism. We no longer have an unbiased media. We have a media that is controlled by a powerful elite that no longer reports the news but manages the news like Big Brother in Orwell's *1984*. However, most people in this country are not aware that this is happening. As such, they are not fighting the spread of totalitarianism by their vote and participation in the governmental process.

It is not too late! If Christians, Jews and other concerned citizens begin to recognize that democracy is in danger, things can be done to preserve freedom and protect our nation. I do not believe that the future is fixed in some fatalistic manner. God has given us the power to choose our own destiny.

In Steven Spielberg's movie *Back To The Future,* the director Robert Zemeckis shows us how our actions, good or bad, influence the future. Our choices *now* produce the future *later* and even small choices can have profound effects in the future. In *Back To The Future II* we see what happens if an evil character named Biff gains certain information and power. Because Biff has certain information, he also now has the power to create the future as he wants it. Since Biff is evil, he turns a beautiful hometown into a decadent super Las Vegas where he runs a corrupt gambling casino empire with crime and prostitution.

In the old Frank Capra classic *It's A Wonderful Life* with Jimmy Stewart we see a similar theme. Jimmy Stewart, who is a good man, begins to feel that his life doesn't count. Then through the intervention of an angel, Jimmy Stewart sees what his town would have become if he never existed and we are shocked to see a quiet town become totally evil and roisterous.

In both *Back To The Future* and *It's A Wonderful Life*

we   see the powerful results of individual choice. We understand how our present actions create the future—good or bad. Right now in America *the future is still up for grabs*. The question is, who will create the future? those who believe in love, God, and goodness or those who believe in self, power, and hedonism?

In the following pages I will outline what could possibly happen in two different scenarios, (1) what will happen if those who believe in love, God, and goodness create the future? and (2) what will happen if those who believe in self, power, and hedonism create the future?

Scenario I: the Future Created by Those Who Believe in Self, Power, and Hedonism

If the present level of apathy among people who believe in love, God, and goodness continues, this is the future we will soon inherit. First of all those individuals who are actuated by self, power, and hedonism typically do not have a well-defined image of God. They usually redefine the real God out of existence as some mystical ball of energy or higher consciousness. In so doing they become as gods since they believe that all is one. Although there are some in this group who still hold to a purely secular humanistic materialist view point, this latter group now represents a small minority.

As such, the people who believe in self, power, and hedonism do not always readily admit it. Nevertheless, when stripped to its bare essentials this is their real belief. Such is the case when media mogul and Cable News Network founder Ted Turner announced that he thought the Ten Commandments should be replaced with a new humanistic ten commitments. Often, those who do not believe in the true, personal, living God of the universe will replace the true God with their mystical god.

This is precisely what happened in the French Revolution. The romantic notion that man is inherently good was a noble idea but it crashed and burned because it was a revolution built on a myth.

Often those who subscribe to elaborate conspiracy theories and ideas about satanic plots completely miss the point. History demonstrates to us that rarely do people choose evil as evil. People think they are choosing good and end up being seduced by evil along the way. All men and women including those who believe in self, power, and hedonism are still created in the image of God. Even in rebellion from the laws of God they conduct themselves as creatures with some kind of law operating in them. The atrocities of both Hitler and Stalin did not start out that way. Both Hitler and Stalin began as agents of what people thought were good political movements. The German and Russian people did not openly vote for dictatorship and totalitarianism. However, wrong choices ultimately produced the horrors that came later.

In the same way, the people in our nation who are moving us toward self, power, and hedonism will find themselves betrayed and in slavery. For example, the mass media in our nation, which is so bent on destroying Christianity and Christians, will eventually find that the emerging secularist super state will ultimately demand from them the relinquishing of their journalistic freedoms.

Therefore, all the choices that are being made now such as outlawing pro-life demonstrations, making prayer in schools illegal, and eradicating Christianity from our society (while at the same time increasing the power of the federal bureaucracy) will eventually produce totalitarianism. It's happening already across the nation. Secular humanism has produced moral anarchy. There are no longer absolutes such as right or wrong. We live in an age of moral relativism. The universal values that at one time evoked respect—the True, the Good, and the Beautiful—have become nonsensical terms within the relativistic structure.

Why are we surprised when desperate young people out of our inner cities join gangs and become violent? As a society, we have brainwashed them into believing there is no God and there is no hope. Consequently, it is predictable that anarchy and violence will be the result. Is it any wonder that the "gang bangers" of the inner cities are dealing drugs and machine gunning people in the streets? Furthermore, since secular humanism always produces moral anarchy, the secular humanistic state can only govern people by force and police power.

The humanists who wail about personal freedom are the ones who will finally produce political oppression. Moral anarchy produces violence and crime. In order to control violence and crime, increased government power must be introduced to keep law and order. As such, totalitarianism spreads rapidly as a means of keeping law and order.

It is already happening in America at lightning speed. Airports X-ray baggage and passengers are searched going on planes, government agencies monitor your expenditures via computer, agencies such as TRW keep electronic files on everybody with a social security number, in the large cities, police helicopters fly over our houses, surveillance cameras monitor us in most retail establishments and on and on it goes. Big Brother is already here and he is getting bigger. The trend will continue as curfews are introduced in major cities and the government steps in to take increasing control to keep law and order.

As the sociopolitical trends continue, Christianity will find itself pushed to a very small corner of society. New laws will strip religion from all facets of public life. "In God We Trust" will be removed from our currency, manger scenes and pictures of Christ will be illegal in schools and public places so as not to offend anyone. All religious meetings will be outlawed on school grounds and in middle class neighborhoods. Bible studies and prayer meetings will require a permit as neighbors who have been indoctrinated in anti-Christian bias via the media will object to the sounds of Christian hymns and people parking near their homes.

Contraceptives will be given out free at every school, homosexual guidance counselors will be available at every junior high, high school and college. Soap operas on television will feature full frontal nudity and explicit sex. Rock 'n' roll groups will openly sing X-rated lyrics. Satan worship will be a legal and established religion as long as human and animal sacrifices are not performed. New electronic drugs will be sold that will get people high via electrodes and allow them to instantly come down with a flick of the switch. All forms of Judaism and Christianity will be openly mocked on film and television and will escalate to the point until Jews and Christians become the most hated people in society (as the Jew was in Nazi Germany).

Finally, practicing Christians and Jews will be arrested and sent to prisons and psychiatric hospitals for re-conditioning. Others will be sent to death camps. All churches will become illegal except for state sanctioned churches. Abortion will be rampant and the mass killing of the elderly or euthanasia will be an accepted practice. Old people will be given pills that put them to sleep and in a state of euphoria forever! In fact, all those with deformities and serious birth defects will be terminated soon after birth.

Society as a whole will be governed by a powerful elite

under the facade of democracy. Corporations will use sophisticated mind control techniques to influence employee productivity. The government will use subliminal suggestions, Skinnerian conditioning, drugs and forms of brainwashing to control people and deal with deviant behavior such as Christianity, addiction, and violence.

On the economic level, all buying and selling will be totally monitored by the government via computer. Your financial transactions will be regularly reviewed by government employees. As such, the new bureaucracy and excessive government regulation will seriously curtail economic growth. Although prosperous in some areas, the new economy will produce some serious shortages and in general a lower standard of living.

As a consequence to this totalitarianism, an underground Christian and Jewish resistance will develop. Bibles will be secretly published, religious television, publishing, and record companies will be non-existent. All major evangelical denominations and synagogues and Catholic churches will fold unless they agree to a government sanctioned theology. Underground Bible studies will spring up across the nation, evangelism will spread rapidly as the new totalitarianism will create great dissatisfaction in the hearts of the people. Both Jews and Christians will be persecuted, arrested, jailed, and eventually exterminated for the public good.

Scenario II: the Future Created by Those Who Believe in Love, God, and Goodness

If the people who believe in love, God, and goodness begin to turn from their apathy and become involved in society and participate in the democratic process, the tide of totalitarianism can be reversed. Although there will be continual confrontation and opposition, America can be preserved as a democracy and a place of religious and personal freedom.

In this scenario, mass prayer, intercession, and repentance will ensue. A new Great Awakening and revival will occur that will flood the churches and synagogues with people returning to God and their religious roots. Through the democratic process, elected representatives will be put into power.

The sexual revolution of the 1950s and 1960s will be checked with family, fidelity, and pro-marriage values becoming fashionable. The moral tide can turn. Television and films will begin to produce works that hold a high view of humanity. In this scenario the influence and spread of pornography will be checked and driven underground where pornographic magazines like *Playboy* and *Penthouse* belong.

In the educational system the theories of creationism and evolution will be taught side by side. Students will be free to choose which theory has the weight of evidence on its side. Manger scenes, statues of Christ and the Ten Commandments will be protected by the government and allowed in public places such as schools and city buildings. Religious assemblies in schools will be protected by the Constitution and both prayer meetings and Bible studies will be allowed on school property.

The federal government's power will be curtailed and no longer allowed to interfere in the religious liberties of the people. Elected representatives who have been elected by the people will begin to enact laws and legislation that, not only protects freedom of religion, but encourages laissez faire economics.

Churches and denominations birthed or rebirthed in the

fires of revival grow and powerfully affect their communities and local populations. A great outflow of compassion and concern begins to flow into the inner cities, the homeless, and the growing Third World, Pacific Rim, and European populations who have made the United States their home.

A rebirth in the original American vision is kindled and a new generation of young people are captured with a fresh sense of the democratic and spiritual ideals that built our nation. Although there will still be tremendous resistance from militant secular humanists and those who have embraced a mystical vision of America (Planned Parenthood, People For The American Way, and the ACLU), a revival in the religious traditions that birthed our nation and the guiding principles of our founding fathers will have captured the imaginations of this New America.

This New America where Christianity and Judaism will flourish will not be a repeat of the original America. This new America or America II will embrace the new populations and cultures which have now made America its home. America II will accept and nurture the Afro-American, Hispanic, Oriental, European, and other cultures. Like the bridge of the *Enterprise* in the movie *Star Trek,* the United States can become a united group of diverse nationalities and cultures moving toward a common goal.

The New America will not be an all white Norman Rockwell painting. The New America will be birthed out of Judeo Christian values, which in their essence believe that all races and nationalities are children of God!

What the Statistics Are Saying

According to a recent survey by the Barna Research Group, four out of five American adults describe themselves as Christian and there are forty times as many churches in the United States (350,000) as McDonald's hamburger stands. Yet, according to Barna *most people see the church as an outdated institution with little to offer a contemporary person.*

The research indicates that only 38 percent of Americans believe that their church is relevant and that only 40 percent turn to God in rough times. In addition, while 75 percent believe that it is important to read the Bible only 42 percent do so at least once a week with other Christians.

The bottom line is that Americans think the Church is out of touch with reality and irrelevant. Ironically, if we contrast those statistics with the New Testament model for church growth we find the exact opposite. In Acts we read about the explosive growth of a true biblical church.

> And everyone kept feeling a sense of awe; and many wonders and signs were taking place through the apostles . . .
>
> . . . praising God, and having favor with all people. And the Lord was adding to their number day by day those who were being saved. (Acts 3:43,47)

In the book of Acts we see the true model of the true church. A sense of awe surrounded the church and miracles were taking place. The church had the favor of the community, and people were being saved. This resulted in explosive growth. Clearly, the American church that the Barna Research Group was talking about was not the same kind of church that the Bible talks about.

The problem in America is that we have churches that are not based on the biblical model. In fact, the above mentioned passages from the book of Acts upset some people's theology. Obviously, if people's theology is upset by the Bible, then it needs to be upset. The data suggests that this American church is in need of both reformation and revival.

Often, the reason young people are flocking by the millions to the New Age movement, Eastern mysticism, meditation, cults, and human potential movements like Werner Erhard's Transformational Technologies, Lifespring, and Scientology is because when they investigated the Church it was irrelevant!

The problem is not with God or Christianity. The problem is that the majority of churches in this nation are not operating on the biblical model. There are some weird hybrids of existential theology, psychology, and humanism that denies the supernatural power of God. They also deny the authority of Scripture. In addition, it is not just one theological camp that has problems. There are exploding evangelical, fundamentalist, and charismatic churches—as well as declining churches in all of these groups—where the Word of God is not upheld and the power of the Holy Spirit is not relied on.

Specifics in Resistance

The following are key areas where people who believe in Judeo-Christian values will have to confront the New World Order.

Politics

Notwithstanding the influence of the mass media and organizations like the Trilateral Commission, America is still a democracy. If those who believe in family values will vote and get involved in local and national politics, we could turn things around rapidly. Organizations like Beverly LaHaye's Concerned Women for America are to be commended for intelligent activism as in the creation of their Crisis-Pregnancy network and should be supported. Not only is Concerned Women for America protesting abortion, but they are offering an alternative.

There are other examples of intelligent political activism: attorney Jay Sekulow of C.A.S.E. obtained a 9-0 victory before the U.S. Supreme Court that upheld the rights of Jews for Jesus and others to pass out religious literature and also won an 8-1 decision favoring Bible clubs in Westside Community Schools vs. Mergens. Jay Sekulow says "passive Christians allow the world to set societies' standards. If we are to turn the tide and win the war, we must begin to do battle now."

Other examples of intelligent activism include John Whitehead's work with the Rutherford Institute and their lawsuit against the federal government for funding the National Endowment for the Arts and supporting anti-family pornography.

Involvement in politics should transcend mere partisan politics. It is dangerous to simply merge Christianity with right-wing and Republican causes. Christians should support any candidate who stands for biblical morality. People who support traditional values have a real chance of winning against extreme liberals if they fight with integrity and vision.

It is an indictment on the Judeo-Christian community and indication of apathy that gay activists who represent only 2 percent of the U.S. population can marshall so much political clout. People who believe in God and morality comprise around forty million people. We have not been nearly as politically effective as we could be.

In June 1969 in Greenwich Village, a gay bar was invaded by police and the Gay Liberation movement was born. This began the Mattachine Action Committee. From that point on gay activists have managed to turn their small numbers into a powerful lobbying force that has real influence in politics and the media. The reason they have been successful is that they have practiced the biblical principle in at least one area: they have been diligent. Proverb states that "the diligent shall bear rule and the slothful shall be under tribute." In politics, gay activists have often been more diligent than Christians in organizing and applying pressure to political leaders.

Although oppressed, the Christian community has not been galvanized into action. For example: when the police arrested a Baptist pastor, in Nebraska; when *The Last Temptation of Christ* was shown around the country; when prayer was taken out of the schools and almost weekly with Operation Rescue, etc. The Church should have been provoked to action. There is still widespread apathy within the Christian culture despite notable heroism. One wonders what is being taught from the pulpits and seminaries of America that allows Christianity to be so interwoven with apathy. What is needed is a new biblical reformation and revival.

There is hope for the future but massive mobilization must happen before it is too late!

The Moral Obligation of Citizenship

It is common on Election Day for approximately one third of our eligible voters to vote. In fact, during a recent election political experts said that we had the worst turnout in fifty years.

According to Sanford Horwitt, director of citizen participation at People for the American Way, "The decline in voting . . . signifies a growing disconnectedness of millions and millions of people who are no longer citizens in any meaningful sense of the word."[1]

Political analysts believe that voters and non-voters are

divided into two groups: *information rich* and *information poor*. They believe single issue politics such as abortion and ecology can have dramatic effects on elections. Also, statistics indicate that younger people vote in fewer numbers than older people.

As voter turnout diminishes, the effect of a smaller minority on the electoral process will increase. Citizens who are concerned about a responsible government and the preservation of the Constitution, as it was originally written, can exercise a real affect on the political process.

It is unconscionable that anyone who is interested in changing our society for the better would not participate in the right of citizenship by not voting. All things considered, we still live in a participatory democracy to a large extent and have the power of the ballot box. God has made us stewards of our country. What we have allowed to become the laws of our land, we will one day answer for.

In an article for the Rutherford Institute, author and director Franky Schaeffer writes about the poverty of trying to transform society with mere conservative, social, and economic principles. Unfortunately, much of the right wing or conservative movement in this country has fallen into such a trap. They cannot understand why people and young people especially have not been inspired by their cause.

Schaeffer is a visionary and defies easy categories. He is an orthodox Christian when it comes to the inerrancy of Scripture. Franky Schaeffer has authored such books as *Sham Pearls for Real Swine*, *Addicted to Mediocrity*, *A Time for Anger* and *Bad News for Modern Man*. In addition, he has directed over four feature films including "Wired To Kill."

The Film Industry

As a former independent film producer walking

through the hotel corridors of the American Film Market, I distinctly remember asking myself why there was no visible Christian presence (not that Christians would be visible by physical appearance). But judging from the amount of horror, sex, and violence in the movies being produced, it was obvious that there was little salt here in Hollywood.

I remember standing in the lobby of a prestigious Beverly Hills hotel as limousine after limousine pulled up with producers, stars, and film buyers from around the world. The lobby was filled with people like Roger Corman, king of the B pictures, and movie stars who were here to sell their latest films. Nowhere amidst this galaxy of movie makers was even a single company that championed family or spiritual values.

It's ironic that the most powerful means of communication ever invented would be totally ignored by those who want to reach the world for Christ.

I   also remember going to events like the former FILMEX FILM FESTIVAL where documentaries, social issues, and arts oriented films were displayed from around the world along with their writers and directors. FILMEX was a serious international film festival for people who loved the art of filmmaking. Here too amidst the hundreds of films on ecology and every social issue and cause under the sun there was no evidence of a single film that represented a biblical world view in even the remotest sense.

Here at FILMEX, one was in the real world. These were the movies that would be distributed for television, theatres, and videocassette around the world. Yet, a visible Christian witness was totally absent. How terrible when one thinks of the hundreds of Christian colleges equipping young people to reach their world. Does not one of these Christian colleges have even a modest film department?

Where were the young, bright, and intelligent Christians? Film should be used to depict and convey a message.

There is a great travesty represented here. The retreatist posture promoted by an evangelical culture that encourages their young people to live in some kind of pseudo spiritual bubble divorced from reality has caused serious problems in our society.

One hears criticism about Hollywood and the kind of films being made. Yet, the Christian culture has not only suppressed the artist and filmmaker from its midst, but it has exacerbated the problem by not encouraging young people to make movies and by not developing young movie makers in their schools.

I can think of several efforts by major Christian organizations to produce movies for theatrical release. Yet, these movie are doomed to failure. The majority of the people involved in making them, with the exception of the director, do not love films. To make movies you must understand the medium of films, you must love the celluloid process and be immersed in the production of films. You must view hundreds of movies and study them and observe what makes movies great. This is entirely absent in evangelical circles, which only want to make movies for utilitarian or propagandistic purposes.

Martin Scorcese, who directed *Last Temptation of Christ*, is a great filmmaker who loves movies. I do not agree with Scorcese in the *Last Temptation of Christ*. In fact, I joined hundreds of thousands of others in picketing Universal Studios because I believed that Universal Studios was attacking the religious beliefs of Christians in unprecedented arrogance and disdain. Yet, Scorcese is revered as a great filmmaker because he has studied the art of filmmaking.

Unfortunately, the evangelical culture has produced

little in the way of great films. As such, to criticize more
effectively, we should offer an alternative. If we are going
to resist the philosophical premise of a New World Order,
we are going to have to produce a culture that aggressively
promotes the arts and film.

Until that time comes, we are going to have a pietistic
culture that can only stand on the outside of society and
bitterly resent it. It's not just a matter of money. It's a matter
of artistic vision and integrity. The gay culture has a film
tradition and actively encourages homosexual filmmakers
such as Rob Epstein and Richard Scmiechen, who made
The Life and Times of Harvey Milk. The black culture has
produced filmmakers like Melvin Van Peebles and more
recently Spike Lee who not only make films for the black
community but stand to protest racism and dare to speak
out for the black culture.

In terms of serious films which ask the really important
questions of life, the evangelical culture is found wanting.
They usually produce manipulative and arm twisting films
about end time prophecy and offer shallow answers about
life.

The really provocative spiritual movies of our day
come from people like Woody Allen who directed *Crimes
and Misdemeanors,* which asks fundamental questions
about morality and the existence of God. Even pictures like
Ghost and *Flatliners* do more to raise questions about
God's judgement and the existence of an afterlife (despite
bad theology) than the majority of Christian films. In the
cultural arena, movies like *The Dead Poets Society,*
Chariots of Fire, and *Godfather III* deal with relevant
themes. These movies demonstrate that society is groping
for answers.

When asked about his belief in God, Jerry Zucker, the
writer of the movie *Airplane,* and the director of the film

Ghost answered, " . . . I'm Jewish and I believe in Judaism.
. . . Judaism brought us ethical monotheism, which is the
belief in one God who demands ethical behavior from us.
I believe it makes a difference whether we are good people
or whether we do evil . . . That's what worries me about
some of the New Age prophets and Shirley Maclaine-ism,
is that it's spirituality without ethics, without belief in one
God that demands morality. . . . Obviously, the portrayal
(in *Ghost*) is very Judeo-Christian."

Ecology

Now we come to the dirty word in some people's
vocabulary as if ecology was synonymous with a leftist or
illuminati conspiracy to control the world. It is true that
organizations like Greenpeace have hidden political agendas. But, ecology should be a Christian issue because it is
a biblical issue. God called us to be stewards of the earth
and not to abandon the earth while waiting for Armageddon. We lose credibility with a secular world because of
our irresponsibility in this area. All true Christians should
be concerned about the environment.

Environmental issues should not be the exclusive
domain of the late Abbie Hoffman, Greenpeace, or
musicians like Sting.

The Inner Cities

The inner cities of America are exploding with gang
violence. This is a nearly deserted mission field of the
evangelical church. It also causes the Church to lose
credibility and favor with a cynical and secular world that
sees us as a community of people who mouth platitudes
about compassion while actually doing very little about it.

In Isaiah, God very clearly warns His people of the
dangers of a lack of compassion.

> Is this not the fast which I chose, to loosen the bonds
> of wickedness, to undo the bands of the yoke, and
> to let the oppressed go free, and break every yoke?
> Is it not to divide your bread with the hungry? And
> bring the homeless poor into the house; when you
> see the naked to cover him; and not hide yourself
> from your own flesh? Then your light will break out
> like the dawn, and your recovery will speedily
> spring forth; and your righteousness will go before
> you; and the glory of the Lord will be your rear
> guard. (Isa. 58:6-8)

Here we see that ministering to the poor, homeless, and oppressed is associated with revival. Could it be that reproach (which the evangelical culture has experienced in our day) is related to its disobedience in these areas?

Franklin Graham's Samaritan's Purse, Charles Colson's Prison Fellowship, and the thousands of local Christian churches that are involved in such ministries are to be commended. Ministries like Rev. E.V. Hill's soup kitchen and ex-football star Rosey Grier's ministry to youth are excellent examples of urban outreach. But, these kinds of ministries must be increased a thousand fold.

Also, the Christian Broadcasting Network's Operation Blessing, which distributes food, clothing, and provides shelter for needy people across the nation, is a living example of the prophet Isaiah's admonition to the church. Organizations like World Vision and the Union Rescue Mission in Los Angeles are other positive role models.

Chapter Six

The Need for Leadership

Television

Television is one of the most powerful mediums of communication in the world. There are a number of excellent programs on television: PBS, CNN, CBN/Family Channel and the networks. However, the majority of programming across the entire spectrum lacks any real meaning or substance. The primary purpose of television is to be a kind of electronic drug, endlessly titillating the audience with nothingness and regular doses of sex and violence.

The real evil of television is not sex or violence. Its true danger lies in its ability like marijuana or tranquilizers to create a kind of brain death and desensitivity to life and relationships. Just walk around any neighborhood in American after dark and look into the windows. You will see the flickering glare of television sets consuming the consciousness of the viewer. This is television's real evil! The fact that it has become the centerpiece of the American living room and instead of talking or sitting on a porch and watching the stars and thinking about life, people now sit hypnotized in front of a picture tube like some kind of electronic dream machine.

The challenge before society is to create an intelligent alternative to television—programming that gives to the viewer the tools to live better. Not programming that takes from the viewer and erodes our basic values for the sake of ratings.

Unfortunately, Christian television with the exception of CBN and some good Bible teachers and preachers is often no better than its secular counterpart. Religious programming is awash in silly, manipulative, and primarily mindless programs that actually prevent the communication of the Gospel in our nation.

When a secular society occasionally tunes in to Christian television out of curiosity, they are often not evangelized. What they see reinforces their worst fears about religion. They do not see an alternative, and even worse, they believe on the basis of what they are seeing that biblical Christianity is a form of madness.

Furthermore, much of Christian television programming is out of touch with the culture. It often does not speak to the people who are watching "In Living Color," "Arsenio Hall," "MTV" and "The Simpsons."

"Television does not reflect our culture anymore, it is our culture . . . " (Neil Postman Author and NYU Professor)

Christian television must begin to speak to contemporary issues if it is going to be relevant.

In Light of Possibilities

We live in a universe where we have been given the power within certain limitations to create enormous possibilities. Nowhere is this more true than in the arena of art, literature, film, and television. The possibilities of communicating through film and television the richness, majesty, and splendor of a created universe originated by a personal, living God of the universe are endless and largely untapped.

Many complain about the steady barrage of meaningless titillation being offered on the networks and cable. But, those who believe in a Judeo-Christian world view have offered little in the way of an alternative. Money is not the problem—vision is.

Imagine a new kind of programming coming from a culture that is dedicated to presenting a Judeo-Christian world view.

Bill Moyers did an interview with a Jewish filmmaker, Pierre Sauvage, who directed "Weapons of the Spirit." It was a brilliant and sensitive portrayal of a community of European Christians who hid Jews at great personal risk from the Nazis during World War II. After the movie Bill Moyers interviewed Pierre Sauvage over the national PBS system. They talked in depth about how faith in God and the Bible equipped these people to withstand the oppression of the Nazis and the wondrous relationship between those of the Jewish and Christian faith. This is the kind of programming that changes the hearts and minds of men.

I am currently attempting to raise the funds for an alternative type of production entitled "Window to the Universe," which would illustrate the three primary world views held by people in the world today (1) The materialist/secular humanist (2) The New Age/Eastern mystical, and (3) The Judeo-Christian world view. The purpose of this production would be to present these three world views before the audience in an entertaining manner and let the audience choose on the basis of a non-propagandistic presentation. This would be done in the confidence that when truth is presented in a non-manipulative and credible manner most people will opt for truth.

There are so many creative possibilities available to communicate sensitively and intelligently the reality of a Judeo-Christian world view.

Sympathy for Frank Zappa

Frank Zappa, the avant-garde musician, who founded the rock group The Mothers of Invention and created Barking Pumpkin records, has vigorously attacked all groups wishing to censor or clean up rock 'n' roll music. Although, not totally agreeing with everything Zappa stands for and thinking Zappa somewhat naive regarding the good intentions of the rock music industry, I would have to sympathize with him in some respects.

First of all, I grew up listening to the Mothers of Invention and enjoyed some of his songs like Suzie Creamcheese. Zappa is a highly creative individual who believes in art and creativity.

Frank Zappa takes one look at some of the plasticity and fraud inside the Christian culture and wants to run for the hills. Christianity is truth and not religion. Let's face it, there is a lot of man made and non-biblical baggage in this culture that is indefensible. If you rub an artist's nose in that (or any thinking person) and tell them this is God, you are going to produce a violent and rebellious reaction. You are going to turn people from God and it is not God they are rebelling from but the nonsense done in God's name.

On the other hand, I think Frank Zappa is very naive if he totally defends the rock music industry. The bottom line of rock 'n' roll music today is, not art or creativity, but money. Payola scandals and an entire industry of executives who will do anything to make money, including corrupt values of the younger generation, are rampant. This is indefensible.

Yet, rock 'n' roll and popular music in general defies categories of good and bad. For example, on one hand you have the clearly prurient work of someone like Billy Idol. He produced a rock video entitled "Rock the Cradle of Love." It is a message of total promiscuity and a plea for giving in to any sexual urge. Or you have Madonna who in her "Justify My Love" video leads the viewer through the world of kinky sex, S & M, and pornography. These are not the types you want to have as a role model for young men and women. It is moral irresponsibility.

Groups like Motely Crew have a new album out called "A Decade of Decadence." Ozzie Osborne sings praises to the satanic priest Aliester Crowely (also known as the Beast). Songs that glorify death, destruction, the occult, and suicide are rampant among certain groups.

Yet, popular music also contains the beautiful and legitimate expressions of love, social protest, and the spiritual search for God. A number of heavy metal style rock 'n' roll groups have recorded songs and videos that are quite beautiful and powerful as prayers to God. For example, Poison has a song that is the cry of a young man who is looking to God for answers; and if you listen carefully, it is the cry of an entire generation looking for God but confused. Another group, Styx, also has a song that is a prayer, entitled "Show Me the Way," which contains the line "Every nite I say a prayer in the hope there's a heaven." Both of these songs are in reality rock 'n' roll prayers or contemporary psalms of a wearied generation tired of meaningless sex and looking for answers.

M.C. Hammer's powerful "We Got to Pray" is a rap style celebration of prayer to Jesus Christ. Jesus is presented as the answer to all of life's problems. These are examples of legitimate contemporary spirituality.

The Need for Artists

My wife Kristina and I drove up the coast of California and stopped at Big Sur. The huge trees and forests were nestled above the high cliffs and the Pacific ocean was a breathtaking sight. Here, nestled in the forest of Big Sur, was the home of the late Henry Miller, the controversial artist whose life is featured in the first NC-17 rated movie, *Henry & June*, directed by Philip Kaufman. We stopped to visit the home that had been turned into a library and museum.

It was a modest cabin-like structure where the artist and author spent his final years. Although I do not share the hedonistic philosophy of Miller nor the emphasis on sensuality that dominates so much of his work, I appreciate the fact that Henry Miller was committed to his art. I couldn't help but think while walking through Miller's home in the woods of Big Sur that the Christian culture is sadly lacking in artists.

Recently, the notorious author and artist William Burroughs held an art exhibit here in Los Angeles. Burroughs—who authored *Naked Lunch* and who was a heroin addict, homosexual, and the father of the beatnik generation—was still alive and kicking. He even played the part of a junkie priest in the movie *Drugstore Cowboy*. Again, while not sharing in the hedonistic excesses of Burroughs and not even sharing in his dark philosophy, I couldn't help but think that William Burroughs was far more creative than the predictable religious culture that often denies the creativity of man.

God is the Creator of the universe with a capital C. If we are to reflect His glory, we must be infinitely creative as He is creative. If we are going to win this great cosmic battle for mankind, then we are going to have to be highly imaginative. Artists and creative people must be allowed to flourish in the Christian culture and given the space to grow—not in sinful excess, but neither in some kind of censorial book burning approach.

The God of the universe is a lot bigger than religion. He transcends the confining boundaries of contemporary religious structure without going beyond the structure of His Holy Word. Within the freedom of the Bible and Lordship of Christ is a rich and expansive world waiting to be discovered.

Painters, sculptors, poets, actors, musicians, writers, and dancers must all be allowed to flourish in the kingdom of God, because as creators, they are close to God's heart (the Creator).

Cultural Leaders

Where are the people who say they believe in God? Why does the Christian culture encourage a ghetto like mentality and a policy of isolationism and retreatism? Why is the Church of Jesus Christ hiding out (except to emerge in some kind of protest from afar) while there is a battle raging in our culture?

To reclaim our nation for Christ, we are going to have to stop hiding out in the never never land of pietism and become the salt of society. On every front from athletics to science we need cultural heroes who are publicly identified with the cause of Christ.

This is a generation in need of heroes. The heroes of our culture should be those who believe in God. They do not have to be evangelists or preachers. They can be ordinary people who are concerned and have taken a stand. Ecology, world hunger, child abuse, poverty, and other causes are waiting to be championed by those who love God.

Education

An article in the *San Francisco Chronicle* talked about a San Francisco community college that makes it mandatory for all students to fill out a form that reads "I am. . . . (1) A gay man (2) A lesbian (3) Neither gay or lesbian." The word heterosexual is not even in the picture. While every college has not gone that far, American education has moved into an ultra-liberal posture over the last several decades. Pro-homosexual, pro-abortion, New Age beliefs, and a multitude of blatantly anti-Christian ideas have been encouraged, and Christianity has been censored through lawsuits by organizations such as the ACLU.

What is needed is for people to confront the educational system. You cannot educate people to reject Christianity and then take these people and have them run the government, business, science, and industry and expect social harmony. Christians must confront the current educational establishment in an intelligent manner and create alternatives.

Christians have the right to question and oppose certain curriculum. However, simply running around opposing everything and acting as censors has a very limited strategic value. Christians must *create* alternative courses that are effective in educating young people.

In California one group that has been highly successful in opposing evolution in public classrooms is the Institute for Creation Research. They have intelligently stood for a scientific yet biblical account of creation by assembling a group of prestigious Christian scientists. This is effective because it moves beyond simply criticizing the educational system. It actually challenges it on an intellectual level.

There are eighty-three thousand schools, over fifteen thousand school districts, and 40.7 million students in the United States (with 4 million professional and paraprofessional workers). Obviously, the task of educational reform is enormous. It is clear that students raised in a moral vacuum with no clear concept of right or wrong cannot move into society as good citizens.

The Family—Building Block of Civilization

According to the report *2001: Preparing Families For The Future*, sociologist Paul C. Glick, who was chief family demographer with the U.S. Census Bureau, the following trends concerning the family are emerging.

* Age at first marriage has increased sharply, from 20 for women and 23 for men in 1955 to 24 for women and 26 for men in 1988.

* Two-thirds of couples in new first marriages are likely to divorce or at least temporarily separate.

* Fewer persons approaching middle age have intact marriages. The proportion of 40-year olds not married has risen sharply from 12% in 1960 to 23% in 1988.

* Alternative family forms are increasing. Cohabitating couples have increased from a half million in 1970 to 2.5 million in 1988. The proportion of children born to unmarried mothers has grown from 5% in 1960 to 23% in 1986.

* More young adults are now living with their parents. In 1960, 43% of 20 to 40 year olds were living with their parents, by 1988 55% were doing so.

Clearly, as American family demographics radically change, so too, the Church must respond to the fractionalization and the increased rate of dysfunctional families. Unfortunately, much of the Church is still geared to reaching the sociologically anachronistic family of the Nelsons or "Father Knows Best." Divorce, incest, and single parent families are statistically way up. Therefore the Church of the future must learn how to become the alternative family for the millions of people who have become socially disfranchised from the traditional American family.

Perhaps the single-most disregarded trend in America is loneliness. Loneliness plagues millions of single and married people who, for various reasons, have moved geographically far from their families.

Dysfunctional families and hurting people have explained the overnight success of people like John Bradshaw whose "Bradshaw: On The Family" book and PBS Series have reached millions. These same people have sought to be embraced by the Church and have not found the "family" they are looking for.

The foundational building block of civilization is the family. The decline of the family unit is the single most tangible reason for the increase in crime, the rise of the cults, alcoholism, drug abuse, and child molestation.

Pornography

Pornography is an insidious form of evil that destroys families and has proved to be a dangerous addiction for many. Even on the global level as Christians seek to evangelize eastern Europe they have often found that pornographers are attempting to spread their venom.

Reports from Germany indicate that within days of the Berlin wall tumbling down, all the porno magazines in West Germany were sold. East Germans were buying them up. Jurgen Klebe, the editor of *St. Pauli Nachrichten*,

"Germany's number one lust paper" (as it is called) reported getting seven hundred letters from East Germany a month after the barbed wire was cut.

West Germany's pornographers are basically middle class business people. There are also people such as Beate Uhse, the seventy year old woman, who generates $70 million in revenues annually through her sex shops, blue movie houses, and mail order business. After the Berlin wall fell, she hired thirty vans and printed six hundred thousand catalogs to distribute in East Germany. It is obvious that Christians evangelizing East Germany will have to compete for the hearts and minds of these people.

Here in the United States, pornography is a billion dollar industry. Christians, however, are doing something about it. Dr. James Dobson reports that former attorney general Ed Meese's Commission on Pornography of which he was a member has helped increase arrests around the country.

In fact, the 2 Live Crew group received a guilty verdict in Florida due to the efforts of one Christian lawyer who was willing to challenge the wrath of the media and the record industry in a bold stand for righteousness. Jack Thompson, the Coral Gables attorney who helped convict the group, called the verdict a message that says "the record industry better stop distributing obscene records that degrade women." Thompson is an example of what one man can do if he will stand up for what he believes.

The Sexual Issue

Modern man has rebelled against biblical standards of sexuality at a great price. Biblical Christians are increasingly being pushed to the forefront on this issue. According to Dr. Jonathan Mann, former director of the World Health Organization's Global Program on AIDS, over seven hundred thousand people have contracted AIDS as of this year alone, and over 8 million people have developed the virus that produces AIDS.[1] AIDS has infected over one third of the population in some areas of Africa. In the Bronx, 5 to 12 percent of pregnant women have AIDS. Figures as high as 25 percent have been reported among young men surveyed in Newark, N.J.

America and the rest of the world are paying some very heavy dues for the free sex party promoted in the 1960s. Syphilis and gonorrhea are also epidemic. American teenagers are experiencing 2.5 million cases of sexually transmitted diseases each year. Nearly 20 percent of all AIDS patients are infected as teens. In spite of this, Hollywood actively promotes casual sex with a vengeance. Even mainstream entertainment films like *Lethal Weapon I* and *II* flaunt obligatory and steamy sex scenes between casual partners.

Men like Josh McDowell have done an excellent job in providing answers to young people in the area of sex. McDowell's book *Why Wait?* has provided a biblical apologetic to a new generation. In cooperation with Campus Crusade for Christ, Josh McDowell has taken his *Why Wait?* program to the Soviet Union. It has been met there with enthusiasm. McDowell is an example of an intelligent and creative Christian going into difficult territory. This author remembers McDowell coming to the University of Missouri over fifteen years ago with his *Maximum, Sex, Love and Marriage Seminar,* which ministered to thousands of college students.

Also, Dr. James Dobson and his FOCUS ON THE FAMILY MINISTRY have provided excellent information in the area of human sexuality.

Sexual Catastrophe

The desire for sexual and romantic fulfillment is perhaps one of the most powerful urges within the human personality. Linked to sexual and romantic satisfaction are the core components of the human personality and soul. Sex, love, marriage, and relationships involve the very deepest range of emotions and interplay between the human personality and the spirit.

Our society has lost touch with the multi-dimensional nature of sexual relationships. Sex for the most part has become merely a physical act with the deeper emotions and personality being compartmentalized or separated from the physical act. Naturally, we cannot divide the sexual self from the emotional and spiritual. What results is sexual chaos.

Deeply ingrained in our culture are false messages and beliefs about sex. The pornography and entertainment industries have inculcated our culture with a new mythology of sex that says sexual chemistry and fulfillment are the result of mere physical attraction and expression. In movies you have people first going to bed together and then getting to know each other. Sex has become as common as eating a sandwich. It has lost its sacredness and significance.

Within the human personality is the potential for intimacy, which physical sexual expression cannot satisfy. Sexual intimacy and orgasmic fulfillment may momentarily squelch the fires of lonliness and separation from self, God, and others. Yet, after the pleasures of the sexual encounter subside, the feelings of anxiety and lonliness once again bubble to the surface.

What every man and woman feels in the depths of their souls is separateness and lonliness that produces a powerful drive for intimacy. What men and women are looking for primarily in sex is a deep and profound intimate relationship that will fill the void in the center of their being. This void can only be filled by God and an intimate relationship. It must be built on true spiritual love. Sex is a gift to be enjoyed and not a final integration point that attempts to use sex as the solution to the desire for intimacy.

It is here in depths of psychological and spiritual need that evil has a real chance to gain control in the human personality and culture. Perverting a legitimate need for both sex and intimacy, evil uses the most powerful of human drives and needs as the machinery of human destruction. What results is (instead of true sexual and emotional fulfillment) nothing less than complete sexual catastrophe.

Our culture has been placed in a sexual wilderness. Those who have claimed to champion Judeo-Christian values have retreated where the battle is most intense. We have left the sexual education of our culture to men like Hugh Hefner and Bob Guccione. As a result, there has been no adequate explanation of the physical, emotional, and spiritual benefits of human sexuality expressed according to God's plan.

Instead, monogamy is equated with monotony, sexual abstinence is considered repressive and unhealthy, and now even heterosexual sex is being promoted as a secondary option. In a sense, a new sexual programming based on the belief of whatever feels good do it has become the guiding sexual ethic.

The result is that rock videos like Madonna's "Justify My Love," which is viewed by young people whose minds absorb both the images and lyrics, are now being programmed to accept sadomasochism, homosexuality, and promiscuity as acceptable sexual toys to be enjoyed by consenting adults.

Educational systems now distribute condoms. Organizations like Planned Parenthood give easy access to abortions. We literally have a "Brave New World" of sexuality in which faithful romantic love between a husband and wife is destined to become a distant cultural memory.

What results is a tearing down and destruction of the human personality. True love and intimacy are replaced with people "using" each other like sexual machines. Thus, words like "hitting on" and getting a "piece" reflect a sexual mentality that is consumer oriented. It is devoid of true love.

This results in millions of people with lacerated hearts and pervasive heartache, loneliness, and emptiness. Once the capacity for true intimacy is lost, we see emotional fallout in the lives of hurting generations. Is it any wonder the family is falling apart? When people do get married, it's the wounded with the wounded. It doesn't last.

Finally, the sexual catastrophe expresses itself in over one million abortions each year and the AIDS epidemic. The Academy Award winning film *Common Threads—Stories From the Quilt*, directed by Robert Epstein and Jeffrey Friedman chronicles the lives of those who died from AIDS. The patches symbolize the lives of real men and women who have died of AIDS. It covers fourteen acres. The movie documents the life and death of some of those people.

Unrestricted sexual freedom in our culture has not produced sexual fulfillment. It has produced suffering, pain, and death. The sexual revolution did not bring sexual freedom. It brought the new tyranny of heart break and disease.

The Sexual Apologetic

God created the orgasm! Hugh Hefner, Helen Gurley Brown, and Bob Guccione had nothing to do with it. In our post Christian culture we have divorced spirituality from sexuality with great problems resulting. We must remember that the entire range of legitimate sexual responses from a look in the eyes, romance, and intimate conversation, a walk at sunset, a candlelight dinner, the softness of a woman's breast, the strength of man's body, intercourse, sexual, emotional and physical communion, and the orgasmic climax were all designed by the Creator of human sexuality as rich experiences to be enjoyed by a husband and wife.

Yet, until recently there has not been an adequate sexual apologetic that affirms that God has blessed human sexuality within the parameters of heterosexual marriage. A resulting confusion has occurred in our society especially among young people in regard to the sexual experience.

Graphic sexual images bombard young people from everywhere in our society—images that give confusing sexual messages from a medium that makes sexual relations as common as taking a walk. Consequently, an entire generation's sexual values have been formed by the mass media with divorce, child molestation, the destruction of personalities, and abortion resulting.

What is needed is a powerful voice from a culture that believes in traditional family values and strongly affirms and celebrates sexual activity between married partners. This traditional family culture must speak graphically and intelligently about how to deal with the strong drive for sexuality within the human personality. If they do not, then a hedonistic culture will, and men like Hugh Hefner and Bob Guccione will educate our families about sex.

A false and non-biblical prudery has done much to promote immorality. Through the pulpit, film, books, and television it must be communicated that sex is good and to be enjoyed and celebrated. However, like driving a car, there are certain rules for sexual behavior that the Bible speaks about.

We must talk in intelligent terms to a sexually sophisticated generation. Simply saying that this or that is wrong is absurd. Why is it wrong? What are the specific consequences of such behavior? A truly biblical perspective on sex must be intelligently communicated with an emphasis on the fact that it was God who created sex for men and women to enjoy.

The Need for Intellectuals and Futurists

The soil of secular humanistic and materialistic thought has spawned many intellectuals, visionaries, and futurists. They have grabbed the helm of our culture and are attempting to steer it into the future. Men such as science fiction author Arthur C. Clarke and R. Buckminister Fuller have delved into exploring the possibilities of societal transformation. Fuller was the guiding force of a whole generation of leftist activists and futurists.

In fact, men like designer Medard Gable who authored *Energy, Earth and Everyone: A Global Strategy for Spaceship Earth* developed a whole system of utilizing a Fullerian approach to solving world problems such as the energy crisis. Peace activist Barbara Marx Hubbard, author of *The Hunger of Eve,* was heavily influenced by Buckminister Fuller, Jonas Salk, Herman Kahn, and Abraham Maslow. She has proved to be an influential agent for global change and a one world government. The list is endless of intelligent and dedicated individuals who are steering our society into the future from a materialist world view.

Yet, when one surveys the landscape of those who subscribe to a Judeo-Christian world view, one sees a real poverty in the intellectual life of this culture and a surprising stagnation of visionary leadership that is able to grab the helm and steer society into the future. With some exceptions there is a real vacuum in intellectual visionary leadership.

What we have is a proliferation of pseudo-prophets who make glib pronouncements regarding Armageddon and the end of the world. As a consequence, a highly educated and secular society looks on with justifiable horror as these misguided prophets grasp at every bit of world news and attempt to make it a sign of end time prophecy. What occurs then is a total abandonment by the Judeo-Christian culture of society and the earth. An abandonment which justifies nuclear arms build up, pollution, world hunger, and war with superficial pronouncements regarding the end of the world. This is not to say that there will not be the end of the world nor that biblical prophecy will not come true. For all the prophecies concerning the Second Coming, the Antichrist, and Armageddon, will come true. This does not mean we should run for the hills and wait for the sky to fall. On the contrary, we have been told to occupy until he comes.

Evangelist Billy Graham said he couldn't agree with those who identified Iraqi president Saddam Hussein as the Antichrist: "History tells us that people thought Napoleon was the Antichrist, they thought Mussolini was the Antichrist and they thought Hitler was the Antichrist" said Graham.[2]

Intellectual leaders emerging from a humanistic culture grapple with the real issues of our day. They often win the respect of the culture with their intellectual integrity. Those emerging from the Judeo-Christian culture, all too often, represent that which is ultimately non-biblical, superficial, and shallow.

What is needed in the Church is a new generation of visionaries and intellectuals who embrace a biblical world view and can articulate it. They would become the torch bearers of our culture and provide solutions to the key issues of our day. In terms of prophetic leadership, it may well be that God will raise up men and women who will fulfill this calling. They must be people of the very highest moral, spiritual, and intellectual caliber.

Radical Environmentalism

The whole world watched in stunned silence as Saddam Hussein created an oil spill in the Middle East that dwarfed the Exxon Valdez tragedy. Helicopters mounted with television cameras brought us footage showing miles of oil spill washing over beaches and drowning sea gulls and other wildlife.

Ecological activists across the nation decried the pollution of the planet in what is a growing movement based on legitimate ecological concerns. However, within the ecological movements are the philosophical seeds of a new religion based on Mother Earth and mysticism.

Beginning with the Sierra Club and the Audubon Society, the ecological movement has become involved in what is now termed Deep Ecology or "biocentrism," which questions man's fundamental right to dominate nature. Using Henry David Thoreau, who was perhaps the first radical environmentalist, as their spiritual father, radical environmentalists have parlayed their Walden Pond philosophy into a global political movement now called the Green Movement.

In 1975 author Edward Abbey wrote the novel *The Monkey Wrench Gang*. In it, a group of "ecoteurs" used sabotage to protect the environment. Abbey's *The Monkey Wrench Gang*, inspired the radical environmental movement that has now bloomed.

In his book, *Green Rage—Radical Environmentalism and the Unmasking of Civilization*[3] author Christopher Manes, a radical environmentalist, gives us the world view of the Deep Ecologists, "By indemnifying anthropocentrism as the root of our troubled relationship with nature, Deep Ecology was taking on more than just a dubious moral precept . . . Charles Darwin's *Origin of Species* had already undercut the metaphysical underpinnings of anthropocentrism by displacing the notion of the scala naturae, the Great Chain of Being, which situated mankind in a privileged station above the 'lower' life forms of a divinely instituted world."[4]

The Radical Environmentalists and Deep Ecologists reject the fundamental precepts of Western civilization—man, the unique creation of the Creator, has been given dominion over the earth, not to rape Mother Earth, but to exercise stewardship. On one hand we have certain Christians and capitalists who legitimize the plunder of the planet, either because Armageddon is here and they are going to get raptured, or for profit. On the other hand we see Deep Ecology as a new religion and its worshippers are out to deify nature and radically restructure society.

Ernest Callenbach, editor of a prestigious film journal and author of *Ecotopia* writes of a new utopia that utilizes ecologically sound, high technology and elaborate recycling systems. Theodore Rozak, author of *Where The Wasteland Ends*, calls for a new society built on a post-industrial vision.

These "ecotopians" have gained the ears of a younger

generation who have seen the results of toxic waste, air pollution, and the destruction of our precious forests. Conversely, this new generation has sometimes rejected the Judeo-Christian perspective because they have seen it falsely represented as repressively fundamentalistic, obsessed with death and Armageddon rather than true spiritual life and the stewardship of planet Earth.

Basic environmentalism should not be the exclusive concern of environmentalists. Concern and activism regarding the pollution of our rivers, streams, and air should be on the agenda of all people—if for nothing else, then for survival. The American and global landscape has been ravaged by an exploitation mentality that has pumped pollutants into our food supplies and has become the cause of cancers and other malignant diseases. Damage to the ecosystem and brutality to the environment all around us have diminished the quality of life for every human being.

A true Judeo-Christian perspective recognizes the earth as a gift from the Creator and seeks to take care of it and replenish it. This should encompass livable cities and communities that are both ecologically sound and physically attractive. This ecological mindset should include food that is nutritious and free from dangerous additives, smog free cities, and emphasis on human environments versus the sterile and dehumanizing environments sometimes produced by technology. This lack of humanness can be found in everything from the birthing rooms in hospitals that are cold and sterile to the offices and factories of America, which are designed for machines rather than for human beings. Those who acknowledge the reality of the Creator should express this belief by actively supporting environments that uphold the mannishness of man and do not seek to dehumanize people.

This may seem like a simple matter, but it is far more

revolutionary than that. In an age which pushes constantly to make man into nothing more than a biological machine or a computer number, the most spiritual thing you can do is stand for humanness and the importance of each individual as a unique creation of God. This should affect the way we do business, the kind of education we give our children, and life in the inner cities. Part of the reason we see the ultra-violence in our communities and the rise of things like Satanism is because our culture has lost its basic moorings of community, family, and environment.

Of course the primary pollution is the pollution within man's soul from which all other pollution stems. A true ecology must be concerned with spiritual and moral pollution—the pollution of human sexuality and morality. Concern for the whales and forests should never take precedence over the lives of babies. If we are going to save the whales and the forests, we must also save the unborn children. Ecology in the truest sense of the word must be concerned with man's relationship to both the Creator and the created world.

Science

Carl Sagan recently held a major bash for the mass media in New York. It was replete with food and speeches extolling the virtues of so-called scientific humanism. Sagan is in reality a dedicated activist to the religion of humanism and an advocate of evolution.

Using taxpayers money, Carl Sagan preached his message of humanism to millions of people over PBS on his show *Cosmos*. He asserted that "the cosmos is all that is or ever was or ever will be." Sagan, as a humanist activist, has a hidden agenda which exudes from his book *Cosmos*.[5] Sagan says, "Every nation seems to have its set of forbidden possibilities, which its citizenry and adherents must not be permitted to think about . . . in the United States, socialism, atheism, and the surrender of national sovereignty." Here we see the merging of humanistic ideologies resulting in a hybrid of socialism/capitalism, atheism/non-biblical Christianity, and materialism. Not to mention of course, "the surrender of national sovereignty," which is essential to the establishment of a New World Order. Sagan continues, "We must be willing to challenge courageously the conventional social, political, economic, and religious wisdom."[6] Obviously, Carl Sagan is not interested in being a mere scientist. He is a social engineer for a New World Order based on humanistic philosophy.

Men of Sagan's ilk have the upper hand with the multi-million dollar backing of the Public Broadcasting System, Random House Publishers, and an open invitation to network talk shows. All of this gives him enormous popularity and credibility.

Judeo-Christian scientists and thinkers can challenge the philosophical assertions of men like Sagan. Dr. Henry Morris, founder of the Institute for Creation Research, has assembled a faculty of thirteen scientists with doctoral degrees in science from institutions like Harvard, Berkley, Rice, Minnesota, Penn State, etc. Dr. Morris has even produced films that teach the scientific evidence for Creationism.

The film series *Whatever Happened to the Human Race?* by Franky Schaeffer Productions with Dr. Francis Schaeffer and Dr. C. Everett Koop (former Surgeon General of the United States) is another example of a powerful scientific apologetic dealing with issues like genetic research, abortion, and euthanasia.

However, these efforts and others are merely a drop in the bucket. Those holding a Judeo-Christian world view must become the scientists/activists of our day. They must be of the highest intellectual caliber if we are going to challenge the prevailing intellectual doctrines of our time. Work by social thinker Jeremy Rifkin, author of *Entropy,* and now an expert on genetic research is highly commendable. A scientific apologetic must be raised up across the world. Ironically, in the Soviet Union (which has outlawed the teaching of creationism), there is a tremendous demand for books dealing with the subject of creation science.

Big Business

Many people look at the mega-corporations and big business and throw up their hands in resignation. Some of these corporate giants are unwittingly helping to establish a New World Order. However, as the Bible tells us "giants can be slain." Christians, like their spiritual predecessor King David, can slay the "Goliaths" of our day. One person or a small group of people can change the direction of massive conglomerates.

The Christian Action Council (CAC) recently took on American Express with their own campaign slogan: "American Express Leave Home Without It." CAC took on American Express because it was contributing to Planned Parenthood, which is the leading advocate of abortions in our society. According to Thomas Glessner, CAC director: "Our message to corporate America is stay out and keep out of the abortion business." CAC has been successful in stopping companies like J.C. Penney, Eastman Kodak, and AT&T from funding abortion (to the credit of these companies). Companies who have not yet cooperated are Bristol Myers, Squibb, Citicorp/Citibank, General Mills, and The New York Times Company.

In the Spirit of Daniel

Across the globe, Christians are on the vanguard of

utilizing the new technology for Christ. In Deuteronomy 28:13 it states "And the Lord will make you the head and not the tail: you shall be above only, and not beneath, if you heed the commandments of the Lord your God, which I command you today, and are careful to observe them."

Evangelist Billy Graham has been utilizing high technology to preach the Gospel throughout the world. In England, Mr. Graham was using *Livelink* a satellite television relay that beamed Graham's message on giant screen televisions in St. George's Hall while the evangelist preached live from London. Via *Livelink* satellite Graham will be beaming into two hundred separate locations from Iverness in Scotland, to Redruth in Cornwall and from the Irish Republic and Northern Ireland across to East Anglia.

Heading up the operation is Barry Roberts, a high powered business executive who set up electronic factories overseas for multinational corporations and is now helping Graham. Livelink has been used in France and many other parts of the world.[7]

Another example of cutting edge evangelism is an organization called World By 2000 headquartered in Pasadena, California. It is a joint venture in evangelism between Far East Broadcasting Company (FEBC), World Radio Missionary Fellowship (HCJB), Trans World Radio (TWR) and SIM Radio International (Radio ELWA). According to World By 2000, 276 languages are already spoken by a million or more people and the World By 2000 is already set up to reach 115 of these languages. Their goal is to reach all 276 languages.[8]

A Window of Opportunity

Mega-investor Rupert Murdoch, whose News Corporation is buying up media options on a global scale, believes that the future of mass media lies in "narrow casting" and predicts the further break up of ABC, CBS, and NBC. In the near future most homes in America will get one hundred or more cable and satellite channels. This means a diversity of news information where no one network will exercise an excessive amount of dominance. Thus the opportunity still exists for those with a Judeo-Christian perspective to present alternative points of view.

In 1978 ABC, NBC, and CBS held a dominant market share of 90 percent of the television viewing. By last year that figure had dropped to 64 percent with independents like Fox picking up a collective 22 percent.[9]

Roughly half of all U.S. households can choose from among thirty channels on cable in a process called "fragmenting," which means that programming responds to different viewer profiles. A similar trend is happening in publishing with magazines such as *Readers Digest* dropping down to 16.3 million readers from 18.4 million and *TV Guide's* circulation has dropped over 4 million. Part of the reason for this decline is that nearly three thousand new special interest magazines are produced each year for a "fragmented" market. It is precisely due to this fragmentation process that Christians now have the opportunity to compete in the mass media. It is very difficult to battle monoliths like CBS and ABC but much easier to compete with a CNN. However, a real danger is evident when the same elite group that owned the media in the past rapidly buys up all the smaller fragmented companies. It is now, during the initial phases of the fragmentation process, that those with a Judeo-Christian perspective can make a real impact.

As Los Angeles Goes So Goes the World

Los Angeles is the cultural role model of the world. Its beliefs and habits are exported via the media on a global level. Thus, recent statistics regarding the church by the Barna Research Group gives us a true indication of where all of America is headed. In a given week only 35 percent of Los Angelenos will attend church compared with the national norm of 44 percent. This could indicate that church attendance is on the decline nationally.

Although two-thirds of everyone surveyed believed that there is one holy God who rules the world, only 37 percent thought the church was relevant. According to Barna "Unless people see the church as relevant to their lives—and unless churches can demonstrate this relevance, it will continue to lose ground."[10]

On a national level Protestant churches continue to decline even further. The Evangelical Lutheran Church lost 36,696 members. The Lutheran Church Missouri Synod lost 10,157 members. The Christian Church (Disciples of Christ) lost 13,549. The Episcopal Church lost 6,878. The Presbyterian Church (U.S.A.) lost 38,173. The United Methodist Church lost 69,430. The United Church of Christ lost 17,787 and a host of other churches also reported losses.

In reality, it isn't surprising that these mainline churches—steeped in liberal and non-biblical theology—are losing members. The lifeforce of God has been sucked out of them through non-biblical theology and people can see the emptiness.

Conversely, the statistics on involvement in Eastern mystical practices, reincarnation, the New Age movement, meditation, and so on are sky rocketing. Obviously, there is a great spiritual hunger out there. It's just not being met by a largely apostate Christian church.

A Crisis in Faith in Judaism

According to the Commission on Jewish Education in

North America, large numbers of Jews have lost interest in Jewish ideals, theology, and values. Over 60 percent of the 1 million Jewish children of school age in North America do not receive any training in the Jewish religion.

Many former Jews now believe that historic Judaism is no longer relevant. What is happening in the Jewish culture as well as the Christian culture is symptomatic of the growth of a secular humanistic world view and the decline, in some quarters, of a Judeo-Christian world view.

Growth of New Age Deception

According to Russell Chandler, author of *Understanding the New Age* and *Los Angeles Times* religion writer, the New Age movement and its deception is growing. In 1978 a Gallup Poll indicated that 10 million Americans were practicing some form of Eastern mysticism and 59 percent of school children now believe in reincarnation. Other statistics reveal that 67 percent of all Americans report having psychic experiences and 58 percent believe in ESP.

Over 30 million Americans now believe in reincarnation. The New Age religion continues to grow on a global scale and will become a powerful adversary to the spreading of the Gospel on a global level. In my two books *Supernatural Faith in the New Age* and *Evangelizing the New Age,* I go into detail about the New Age movement as well as my own involvement in Eastern mysticism and my conversion to Jesus Christ.

Re-Inventing America

America is at the crossroads spiritually, morally, economically, and politically. The choices we make now will create our future. Basically, the question is, upon whose vision will the new America be built? Will the new

America be built upon a New Age world view that believes mankind is the product of a random mixture of chemicals in some kind of Darwinian accident? In this philosophical flow one can expect the continual breakdown of the American family with the resultant promotion of homosexual life-styles, abortion, or the French "kill pill," and the emergence of a New World Order. This New World Order will be governed by self-appointed elites that will usher in a new form of totalitarianism. Or will the American vision be built upon a Judeo-Christian world view that reflects the creative vision of the Creator in all areas of life? In this vision of America, real men and women in a real relationship with the personal, living God of the universe can create a brand new America built on the values of the Scriptures. These values that are built upon a vision of mankind as a special and unique creation of an endlessly loving and intelligent Supreme Being would produce a world of racial harmony, ecological paradise, and economic prosperity. In this philosophical flow of things men and women would have the raison d'etre for a culture much like our founding fathers had in mind except broad enough to embrace many nationalities who have fled the tyranny of their homelands in search of a better home.

America was never meant to be a static concept or a fixed idea. America, just as mankind, must grow in order to survive. The critics of what is termed Christian America are right when they dismiss American middle class Christianity as too narrow. American middle class Christianity is wide under the Lordship of Christ. Wide enough to create a new America that embraces our black brothers and sisters, the millions of Hispanics that have crossed our borders, the Iranians who have fled the Muslim dictatorships, the Vietnamese, Cubans, Eastern Europeans, and all who have come to our shores in search of freedom and opportunity.

The movie *Star Trek* gives a wonderful vision of a new America with its sense of adventure and multi-ethnic richness. Those with a biblical world view have a wonderful opportunity to create a new America or to re-invent it. Tragically, many Christians envision a new America as a kind of white Disneyland with the worship of middle class values and the exclusion of God mandated ethnic diversity and creativity. Thus, many rebel from what they think the Bible is all about. But, they are not rebelling against the Bible, they are rebelling against a religious interpretation of the Bible—a perversion of the Scriptures.

We have it in our power to re-invent a new America and to build a brand new world. But this counterculture will not be built on middle class values and two dimensional evangelical Christianity. It will be built on an accurate view of the Scriptures and a creative relationship with an endlessly creative God.

Chapter Seven

Future Christ

Confessions of an Ex-Radical

There was a time when I shared the general consensus of our time and dreamed of what Beatle John Lennon wrote about in his song "Imagine There's No Heaven." His dream of a global unity appealed to me. I grew up in what could be termed, a secular humanistic but loving home. I was matured on the *Sunday New York Times*, art, culture, and political discussion.

For me, biblical Christianity was not even a viable option. I thought that all Christians were ignorant and superstitious. I believed this religion was blood stained, anti-sex, anti-joy, and anti-love. I thought psychologist Eric Fromn was right when he called Christianity a primitive religion, which invented for its own needs the concept of God the Father.

To me, Christianity was the Bible Belt and men wearing dark, three piece suits screaming hallelujah and dunking people in the river. When the sixties counterculture revolution took off, I joined in. At the age of fifteen I joined radical activist Abbie Hoffman in demonstrating and marching on Washington, D.C. In addition, I read Marcuse,

Allen Ginsberg, Alan Watts, William Burroughs, Norman Mailer, and became thoroughly radical.

I spent my free time in high school hanging out in New York's East Village and joining YIPPIE and the Youth International Party. I experienced the counterculture revolution on New York's lower east side. I can remember going to see the Jefferson Airplane and Grateful Dead at Bill Graham's Fillmore East and listening to Timothy Leary on St. Mark's Place.

The 1960s and 70s created a literal explosion of thought and action. It was a time of deep soul searching, sexual experimentation, and spiritual searching. What fueled the sixties was a deep, spiritual hunger reflected in the poetry of men like Gregory Corso and best-selling novelist of *One Flew Over The Cuckoo's Nest* Ken Kesey. The middle class church consisting of neatly dressed men and women sitting in pews looking like participants in Tricia Nixon's wedding were no match for the raw spiritual hunger and pure rebellion of the period.

I too surveyed American middle class Christianity with its churchianity, its boredom, and lack of legitimate miracles. I ran to the gurus like Baba Ram Dass and Stephen Gaskin, founder of the Farm. It wasn't until fleeing a middle class Christian religious retreat on the back roads of Missouri (hitchhiking) that I had a miraculous encounter with the Person of Jesus Christ. It changed my life forever, and I realized that Jesus Christ was God and not some plastic statue plopped on a dashboard of a Chevrolet.

Until then, I was militantly opposed to Christianity and wanted to see a global revolution of consciousness that would usher in a new world order. It was only after accepting Jesus Christ, and understanding that Christianity was Truth and not a religion, that I began to understand that there was indeed a great cosmic battle occurring on planet

Earth. A battle between good and evil or God and the devil and that political, spiritual, and even economic ideologies were direct expressions of this battle.

Once I entered into a personal relationship with the personal, living God of the universe, I understood that history was not just a random collection of events. There was a definite plot with many sub-plots. I understood that the major plot concerned man as a fallen creature. Jesus Christ came to redeem mankind. He shed His blood for the forgiveness of sins. Until that point I did not even believe in the concept of sin. To me, sin was some archaic concept. It was a relic from an ancient belief system. After accepting Jesus Christ, I felt and experienced an acute awareness of my sinfulness as well as the release of the spiritual, psychological, and soulish manifestations and bondages that this sin creates in the human personality.

Who is God?

Christians, Jews, Muslims, Mormons, Hindus, Buddhists, and other mystics believe in a concept of God. The big question is, "Who is God?" If he exists, "What is He like?" and "What is God's character?" It is somewhat strange to me that as a culture we do not publicly ask ourselves this question. There are no television specials on God's existence. I think our cultural silence about God demonstrates our collective fear of Him. Sex is no longer the great taboo in our culture, God is. You can talk about any sexual act on television in pornographic detail. However, if you talk about God in any serious manner, you will be kicked off most television talk shows. If God did not exist, then why would people spend so much energy trying to push Him out of existence?

The reason militant atheists and groups like the ACLU (American Civil Liberties Union) are trying to eradicate manger scenes and any references to God and religion in our culture is because they are reacting to God's existence in the first place. The ACLU and other groups that hate Christianity know deep within themselves that God does exist. The reality is that God exists. People, who either consciously or unconsciously have chosen to oppose God, are frightened of Him and must attempt to censor Him out of society in the same way a person who is addicted to drugs and alcohol must deny the reality of their addiction in order to stay high. Like drug addicts seeking a fix, atheists and humanists must spend much of their energy in denial in order to maintain their false view of reality. Like alcoholics wanting you to drink with them in order to keep them company, those addicted to atheism must remove all references to God in order for you to share their addiction.

God exists and God has a character and definition. God is called the personal, living God of the universe because, like the men and women He created in His image, God has a distinct character and personality. If we were to describe God's personality, we would use the words love, righteousness, creative, and holy. Unlike the Eastern mystical or New Age view, God is not "perfect nothingness," "consciousness," "non-personal energy," nor is God the collective product of our imaginations. God is not non-personal as the mystics, Hindus, and New Age people believe. God revealed the essence of His personality to the human race when He sent His Son, Jesus Christ, to planet Earth. Here we see God's character revealed.

The King of the universe temporarily discarded His royal stature to walk and talk to men in the form of a man—Jesus Christ. God showed us what He was like in Jesus Christ who was loving, humble, compassionate. He raised the dead and cast out demons. Jesus Christ obediently went to the cross and died for the sins of all mankind. Jesus Christ was resurrected from the dead and broke the power of sin and death over the entire human race. In John 3:16 it says, "For God so loved the world, that He gave His only begotten Son, that whoever believes in Him should not perish, but have eternal life."

The personal, living God of the universe came to us as the Son of God—Jesus Christ—the Saviour of mankind. Thus, we can see that the real God is a God of absolute love and that He loves each one of us on a personal level. The infinite God of the universe knows you personally and intimately. He knows your hurts, joys, and dreams. God cares for you like a heavenly Father and wants to embrace you with His arms. God wants to free you and remove your frustrations, bitterness, and disappointments. When we talk about Jesus Christ as Saviour, this is what we mean. We are not talking about Jesus Christ as the Saviour in religious terms. It is not about religion. It is not a list of do's and don'ts. True biblical Christianity is about an intimate one on one relationship with Jesus Christ.

When the Bible talks about believers in Jesus Christ it is not talking about a bunch of people who get together and con each other into believing in God and shout hallelujah. Believers in Jesus Christ are those people who share a common friend in Jesus Christ. They are people who know God and walk with God on a personal level.

Who is God? All that we can know about God is wrapped up in the person of Jesus Christ. Personally, I think it is tremendously liberating to know that each of us is not alone in the universe or in this world. There is no problem too great for God. The incredible news is that we are not in this world alone. It is not "us against the world." If we understand what is really real, we can know that once we accept Jesus Christ into our lives by faith, we can walk with the personal, living God of the universe through all our problems and share all of our joys and victories with Him.

Steven Spielberg captured a little of the feeling of this in his movie *E.T.* He was not alone in the universe; E.T. could phone home. So we can phone home, not to a fantasy figure like E.T., but to a real loving and caring God. This reality is a cause for celebration and rejoicing. It means that as human beings we are free! It doesn't mean that all of our problems will go away. But it means that the way we approach life should be forever changed. Life for the believer in Jesus Christ should become an incredible adventure. Each day should be filled with excitement and challenge as we approach life in the confidence that we are walking in relationship with a good God—the personal, living God of the universe. This reality should blast us out of our victim mentalities or fox hole style of living. The reality of our personal friendship with Jesus Christ should move us to a higher ground of living. It should cause us not to be religious but bold, adventurous people who are living a supernatural life-style grounded in the reality of our relationship to each other and to God.

An Error in Strategy

The contemporary Judeo-Christian culture has made a fundamental error in strategy as it attempts to confront the secular juggernaut—an "out of control" hedonistic and materialistic society. The error has been our attempt to be the moral policemen of the world rather than torchbearers.

Clearly, as Dr. Francis Schaeffer said, the United States and Europe are what can be termed "post-Christian cultures." They no longer have as a philosophical base the Judeo-Christian values of the Bible. Since they are not Christians, you can no longer appeal to them to behave like Christians as did our forefathers. Consequently, when you

stand on the outside of this secular culture and cry out for
Judeo-Christian morality, it is the equivalent of standing in
front of a roaring freight train with a sign that reads repent.
You may get smashed to smithereens. That is exactly what
is happening as moralists rail against the National Endowment for the Arts funding of obscene and anti-Christian art
or the outcry against the "rap group" 2 Live Crew. It is also
happening as Christians speak out against film, television,
and music that is lewd and offensive.

I am not suggesting for a moment that Christians
should stop speaking out against pornography, abortion,
and so on. We are the salt of the earth. We must escalate
these efforts. But, it is a serious error in strategy to stop
there and leave a secular culture with the impression that
Christianity is defined by negatives.

The world and the artistic community know what we
are against as Christians. But what are we for? If a post-
Christian culture looks at our television, film, and music
industry, they would have to say, except for a few notable
exceptions, that we are not for much! The art and creativity
that is produced by the Christian culture is often two-
dimensional, flat, trite, manipulative, and ugly in both
man's and God's eyes.

It is imperative that the Church of Jesus Christ properly
evangelize the visionaries and artists of our culture. This
cannot be done by endlessly crying censorship. It is
precisely due to this failure in strategy that the Christian
culture is experiencing the back-lash from the creative
community. Here in Los Angeles, there are grotesque
billboards of Senator Jesse Helms because of what their
backers perceive as his anti-art stance. In fact, hundreds of
art galleries across the nation are exhibiting art that is
religiously offensive just to get back at what they perceive
are attacks by "Christian fundamentalists." It is no accident

that movies like *The Handmaid's Tale* and books like Thomas Pynchon's *Vineland* deal with themes of right wing persecution.

In order to change the direction of society, Christians must provide moral and cultural leadership; in order to provide leadership, you must have a VISION.

Prophecy, Revelation, and the Flow of History

An important component in understanding current events can be found in understanding the prophecies in the Bible as they relate to modern history. In the book of Daniel during the time of Babylon, we see that Daniel was given a prophetic vision from God concerning the final chapter of human history. In speaking of various kingdoms that will rise and fall upon the earth we read: "As for the ten horns, out of this kingdom ten kings will arise; and another will arise after them, and he will be different from the previous ones and will subdue three kings. And he will speak out against the Most High and wear down the saints of the Highest One, and he will intend to make alterations in time and in law: and they will be given into his hand for a time, times and a half time" (Dan. 7:24-25).

In this passage of Scripture, Daniel is speaking of a far off future time when a kingdom of the Antichrist will emerge. Here we see that the Bible prophetically reveals future events. It must be remembered that the Bible is filled with historical prophecies—none of which have failed to come true at the appointed time. In fact, the coming of the Messiah or Jesus Christ was prophesied many times in the Old Testament in great detail down to how he would be born and how he would be killed. Therefore, due to the absolute historical reliability of the Scripture, we need to pay careful attention to its predictions regarding the future.

In the book of Revelation, the Apostle John reveals a

vision of the future that he received while in exile on the island of Patmos. In Revelation chapter 13 we read an account of a future one world government based on a unified economic, political, and religious system under the rulership of an authoritarian leader called the Antichrist.

The Bible has predicted the concept of globalism, a New World Order, and a one world government centuries before it was ever a tangible concept. It is important to ask the question, "Is it merely coincidental that many in our world are actively organizing and promoting a one world government?" In other words, "Is it simply circumstantial that the scientists and elites in our culture are calling for the establishment of a one world government to solve all of our problems?" It is interesting to note that modern humanistic thought is predisposed toward the same conclusion of a one world government—just as the Bible predicted.

Thus, we have scientists, social activist, Trilateralists, bankers, and politicians scurrying around the world attempting to unite the world for the sake of peace and prosperity. All of these are noble ambitions; however, there is one fatal flaw in the grand design of globalism and economic interdependence. While all the technological, economic, and military systems are being put in place to accomplish this, the lessons of history are once again being ignored.

The philosophical base for this push toward globalism is secular humanism and the idea of the perfectibility of man. The same flawed idea ran through the Renaissance, the Enlightenment, and the French and Communist Revolutions. The concept that man is basically good and that peace and harmony can be realized if we simply re-order society is very dangerous.

The danger is that as the various systems for globalism are put into place, the potential for totalitarianism skyrockets. In addition, this noble idea of Utopia based on humanistic ideals will ultimately fail. There are those individuals and groups waiting in the wings who, in their quest for absolute power and control, will use the naivete of the idealists to bring about their subjugation. It happened in Communist Russia when Marxist idealists were shocked to see the brutality of Stalin and Lenin as they murdered their opponents. It happened in the French Revolution when the followers of Voltaire saw reason trampled. It happened during the movement of the sixties when counterculture idealists saw the revolution turn sour with the emergence of the violent Weather Underground, the Hells Angels, and the Rolling Stones' concert at Altmonte Speedway graphically filmed in the movie *Gimme Shelter*. It happened in the higher consciousness and New Age movements when spiritual pilgrims saw people being dominated by gurus and so-called enlightened teachers; it will happen in the push for the New World Order.

Once the party is over and a New World Order is established, a secretive elite group bent on power and perhaps the Antichrist himself will emerge. He will seize control promising peace and prosperity as did Lenin and Hitler. Mankind and the naive idealists will be betrayed; brutal totalitarianism will rise again. The millions of Jews sent to the concentration camps and gassed to death, the millions Lenin and Stalin massacred, the millions Mao annihilated are all just warm up acts to what could happen if a single totalitarian leader assumes control over the world.

We must realize once and for all that mankind, apart from God, gradually marches into the darkness. The further a culture drifts from God, the darker it can get. We cannot ignore the biblical warning concerning history and the real and present danger of an Antichrist emerging in the future.

Globalism, one world government, and increased controls by hidden elites pave the road to dictatorship no matter how innocent those ideals may be.

The Prophetic Countdown

World events and specifically trouble in the Middle East must remind us of the numerous biblical prophecies that point to the end of the world and Armageddon.

Ezekiel chapter 38 predicts a future invasion of Israel by Russia, Iran, Iraq, and other nations. The prophet Daniel foretells a future ten nation confederacy during the last days (Dan. 7). Some believe this could be the new United Europe. The Apostle John in Revelation chapter 13 predicts the emergence of the Antichrist, a one world government, and a new world religious system. In fact, the Bible is filled with prophetic warnings about the end of the world.

Although I believe that all the biblical prophecies will come true, I have a serious problem with the way these prophecies are being used by many as the rationale for widespread apathy and non-involvement in society's problems.

Prophecy was written to bring men understanding and bring them closer to God. However, the Old Testament prophets, such as Daniel and Joseph, did not sit in the corners of society pointing out with glee the doom about to befall. These men were of the highest, moral, spiritual, and intellectual caliber. They provided both solutions and answers to their culture from God. These supernatural solutions and answers, which God gave them, were designed to bring men closer to God.

There seems to be unabashed approval of the wholesale destruction of the earth as if it justifies their position. As a consequence, men and women are not being brought closer to God; and an unnecessary animosity exists between us and our secular society. What is needed is a new generation of prophets who know biblical prophecies, but who also offer compassion, moral excellence, and solutions as did Daniel and Joseph.

The Prophetic Timetable and the Middle East

The war in the Middle East and Saddam Hussein's invasion of Kuwait by Iraq all seem rooted in the birth place of civilization. In fact, Hussein compares himself to King Nebuchadnezzar and is building a billion dollar palace. It was here in ancient Babylon that mankind first had its dreams of a one world government. It is here where the Tower of Babel was built. It is ironic that centuries later mankind is involved in a conflict with ancient Babylon, the results of which could help to establish a New World Order.

As millions of Americans and people around the world watch programs like CNN and the evening news, it's as if history were repeating itself. With all this focus on the Middle East the nation of Israel is continually in the forefront.

Politicians and multinational corporations scramble to forge the New World Order. Israel was pressured to lie down and play dead so that Saddam Hussein would not be able to marshall support from Muslims and the PLO. As the world's eyes center on the oil rich nations in the Middle East, Israel is increasingly being cast in the role of the bad guy.

It's as if biblical prophecy were coming alive before our very eyes. In Ezekiel chapter 38 we see the Hebrew prophet warn of a far off time when the nations shall gather against Israel in a mighty military invasion, and God will supernaturally destroy Israel's enemies.

Much harm has been done by many who have made

glib prophetic pronouncements regarding the end of the world. However, we would do well to follow the admonition of Jesus Christ when he talked about the signs of His return in Matthew 24:1-27. Among the signs of His return are:

1. There will be many who claim to be the Christ; and there will be an increase in false Christs, false prophets, and spiritual teachers who will show great signs and wonders to mislead people.

2. There will be wars and rumors of wars.

3. There will be an increase in famines and earthquakes.

4. There will be an increase of tribulation and persecution against Christians.

5. The Gospel will be preached throughout the world.

6. There will be a great falling away from the faith.

7. Lawlessness will increase and people's love for one another will grow cold.

Never before in the history of mankind have we seen such an increase in wars, earthquakes, famines, false prophets, false Christs, lawlessness, persecution as well as the preaching of the Gospel on a global scale to all the nations. Although we cannot be sure when Christ will return, we should never use prophetic signs as an excuse for apathy or non-involvement in society's problems. We must live our lives in the awareness that Jesus Christ could indeed return in our generation. Prophecy should spur us on to evangelize and to become involved in feeding the poor, providing shelter for the homeless, ministering in the inner cities, going into prisons and participating in the political process.

The End of the Age

It is clear that the next several decades will be a time of major economic and societal upheaval. It seems as if civilization itself is teetering on the brink of apocalypse. The decades ahead will be a time of unparalleled technological and scientific advance. It will be the best of times and the worst of times.

In the book of Daniel, the prophet Daniel was given a vision concerning the last days of mankind. An angel came to Daniel with the words, "Now I have come to give you an understanding of what will happen to your people in the latter days for the vision pertains to the days yet future" (Dan. 10:14).

Daniel 12:10 says, "Many will be purged, purified and refined; but the wicked will act wickedly, and none of the wicked will understand, but those who have insight will understand." The book of Daniel is dealing with the end of the age, and yet God promises His people wisdom, purpose, and power in the middle of chaos. In contrast, the people who do not know God will be terrified, confused, and in despair.

The next millennium will be a time when "many will go back and forth, and knowledge will increase" (Dan. 12:4). Due to satellite technology and advance air travel, we live in what Marshall McLuhan termed a global village. As the New World Order emerges and internationalism grows, mankind is experiencing an exponential advance in technological and scientific achievement. However, these advances will not be enough to deal with mass starvation, epidemics such as AIDS, nuclear winter, ecodisaster, and the breaking up of the ozone layer producing global warming.

Mankind will launch a desperate attempt to stave off

disaster, spending millions on things like the Biosphere in Arizona and other brave new world attempts at creating harmony in the midst of chaos. At the root of modern man's dilemma is the fact that man, apart from the Creator, does not possess the knowledge and power to order this world. This is the crux of man's problem. He is attempting to run his world without God. It cannot be done. Mankind is not big enough to play God, and that is precisely why the world is crashing in on him.

The book of Daniel states, "And those who have insight will shine brightly like the brightness of the expanse of heaven, and those who lead many to righteousness, like the stars forever and ever" (Dan. 12:3). It is prophesied that in these latter days a tremendous opportunity exists for people who know God. They will be given enormous insight into the future to evangelize and lead people to Jesus Christ.

Religion —the Enemy of Revival

Christianity is Truth and not a religion. Christianity should not be viewed just as religion. Christianity is Truth as it applies to all of life and not just the "spiritual."

Christianity has become just a religion in America, and thus, it has no teeth or cutting edge. In fact, it is viewed by most of its adherents as just another competing religion with Buddhism, Hinduism, or the New Age.

Jesus Christ is God. He rose from the dead in real space-time history. He is indeed the God of the universe. He is not God because we believe Him to be God. He is the true God apart from our beliefs for He is the personal, living God of the universe. Religion is primarily a cultural force while Truth is real power. Our society is sliding into hedonistic chaos. Eventually, totalitarian control will be needed to manage the chaos.

Christianity as a religion is a weak opponent to the evils

of our day while Christianity as Truth can indeed confront society and has the power to change it.

American   middle class Christianity is a safe but ultimately powerless version of New Testament Truth. For either   Christianity is on the cutting edge or it is not Truth—Truth by its very nature is on the cutting edge.

American middle class Christianity, however well-intentioned, is not true biblical Christianity. The Bible is a book about heroes, warriors, artists, missionaries, and leaders who defied the status quo to follow God. Conversely, middle class Christianity subtly attempts to fit God between the pages of what is defined by cultural normalcy.

We must never forget that God is the Creator of the universe with a capital *C* for Creator. This connotes Creativity. Therefore, if we are to truly follow God, we must also be creative. The middle class church by its very nature cannot be truly creative because it is built on the confines of middle class values which unconsciously block out creativity. If God wants to send massive and total revival (which He does), the middle class church resists the intrusion of God's full lifeforce. It does not fit into the neat little package they have created. What will happen, then, is that the roar of society racing toward oppression will become so great that the middle class church will be forced through external pressure to become great, heroic, and creative.

Chapter Eight

Revival & the Armies of Heaven

A Call to Prayer

First of all, then, I urge entreaties and prayers, petitions and thanksgivings, be made on behalf of all men, for kings and all who are in authority, in order that we may lead a tranquil and quiet life in all dignity.

This is good and acceptable in the sight of God our Savior, who desires all men to be saved and to come to the knowledge of the truth.

Therefore I want men in every place to pray lifting up holy hands, without wrath and dissension. (1 Tim. 2:1-3,8)

In this letter to Timothy, the Apostle Paul tells the Church that they can truly affect the political and spiritual environment of their nation if they will be faithful to pray for those in authority. In addition to the power of the ballot box, we have the power of prayer to regulate affairs in our nation.

Our nation is in trouble and sliding down the path of totalitarianism. In addition to being active politically, Christians have the opportunity of transforming their culture through prayer. I am convinced that Adolf Hitler rose to power because the German Church had been weakened through "higher criticism." The theological seminaries and churches began to doubt the authority of God's Word. In addition, the German Church became apathetic and did not assume its divine mandate to intercede for its nation and bind the powers of darkness. As a consequence, the powers of darkness prevailed and Adolf Hitler rose to power.

Although parts of the world will eventually fall into the control of the Antichrist and a totalitarian global government, the spread of totalitarianism is not in some fatalistic divine plan. The Church in the United States may, through the power of prayer and intercession, successfully withstand totalitarianism and preserve democracy in the midst of global chaos. The Bible is clear that God will not desert His people if they are faithful to Him.

The United States is hanging in the balance. During the past decade there has been major thrusts of intercession and repentance. In one national rally, Washington For Jesus, hundreds of thousands of people wept in repentance before the Lord and interceded for our nation.

In the 1970s the Church on the Way in Van Nuys, California, under the direction of Rev. Jack Hayford, spearheaded a national call to intercession in the form of a musical entitled "IF MY PEOPLE." It was based on II Chronicles 7:14, which says, "If my people who are called by my name humble themselves and pray and seek my face and turn from their wicked ways, then will I hear from heaven, will forgive their sin and heal their land."

God spoke these words to King Solomon after he finished building the house of the Lord and the Shekinah

glory of God filled the house. The Shekinah glory of God
was the supernatural manifestation of the presence of God.
The Lord told Solomon that if the people of God were in
trouble, this trouble would be related to their spiritual
condition; if they would repent and seek God, He would
heal their land. This same promise of supernatural
deliverance holds true for our world today. In the 1990s
The Church on the Way continues to be a command center
for global intercession.

America is sliding toward totalitarianism, and a global
elite is attempting to steer society in a godless direction.
The Church of Jesus Christ has been given powerful
weapons of prayer that are far greater than any hidden
agenda the enemies of Christ may have. An article in
Charisma comments on the power of prayer.

Concerts of Prayer

Prayer is the most powerful thing we can do to change
the direction of history. Activism and evangelism without
prayer is useless. In a bold thrust of spiritual warfare, Dick
Eastman created what is called "Concerts of Prayer" to
intercede for our nation. Dick Eastman and others on the
National Day of Prayer Committee, which include Joy
Dawson, Evelyn Christianson, Norvel Hadley and Vonette
Bright, have mobilized a prayer army which has been
following the patterns of revivals over the last 250 years
and have created 124 Prayer Concerts in major cities across
the United States. In hundreds of cities across the United
States Christians have united to intercede for the lost and
break the powers of darkness. In New Orleans 100,000
Christians have united in a round the clock prayer vigil and
the movement is spreading.

The Counter Attack

But now Western Europe is well into its post Christian era and the United States is teetering on the edge. A major spiritual revival coupled with concerted political action by all American Christians may save American society. Without it, the world will in time degenerate first into hedonistic chaos then authoritarian dictatorship. Pour into that cauldron a heavy potion of New Age Satanism and the way could be prepared for an intense hatred of the followers of Jesus Christ with terrible persecution soon to follow. That is why the next couple of years are so absolutely crucial for massive worldwide evangelism and in the United States for concerted prayer and the training and mobilization of Christians for the political and judicial activism needed to secure their rights and freedom.[1]

As we enter this brave new world of the future, prayers and actions will be of paramount importance. It can no longer be business as usual for the Christian Church. Either we have revival and political reform, or we stand to be imprisoned, silenced, and intensely persecuted.

However, there are signs of hope on the horizon. For the first time since 1962, the U.S. Supreme Court has ruled that Christians and other groups have equal access under the law in public schools. Jay Sekulow of C.A.S.E. (Christian Advocates Serving Evangelism) argued the case for religious liberty that has now opened the way for the legalization of Bible clubs and prayer meetings on public school grounds.

Theologian and church growth expert Dr. C. Peter Wagner comments on the mighty *third wave* of the Holy Spirit, which he believes started in 1980 and will culminate with 645 million people by the end of this century.

According to Wagner, the first wave was the Pentecostal movement beginning around the 1960s and is projected to have 222 million followers by the year 2000.[2]

Extraordinary reports of evangelism are happening all around the globe. According to Loren Cunningham, the president and founder of Youth With a Mission, he is sending two thousand evangelists to Eastern Europe and the Soviet Union along with the intercessory prayer-musical production *"IF MY PEOPLE"* with Jimmy and Carol Owens. Cunningham believes that "the walls came down in Eastern Europe and the Soviet Union because they weren't political or ideological walls. They were spiritual walls." He may be right.

> Everyday an estimated 20,000 are coming to Christ in the vast rural areas of China. Nepal had only 6 Christians in 1959. Now despite persecution and imprisonment there are 100,000 believers . . . 12 percent of Indonesia's Muslim believers have become Christians . . . Ten percent of Singapore became Christians in the 1980s while Korea is at least 30 percent Christian—mostly first generation converts from Buddhism. Everyday there are 78,000 new Christians worldwide, and every week 1,600 new Christian churches.

Loren Cunningham concludes by stating: "Will we see the Great Commission fulfilled in our lifetime?" I believe we will. It will cost us everything we have, but we can see the last commandment of Jesus accomplished and the triumphant return of the King of kings!

World Evangelism

The world is becoming what Marshall McLuhan termed a "global village," and powerful unifying forces seek to unite our planet while New Age ideas sweep across the consciousness of a new generation. Global evangelism by dedicated Christians continues undaunted in an effort to fulfill the Great Commission.

Under the banner "Proclaim Christ Until He Comes—Calling the Whole Church, to Take the Gospel, to the Whole World," the second International Conference on World Evangelism or Lausanne II took place in the Philippines with Billy Graham kicking off the plenary session. Over four thousand men and women gathered in an effort to "bring fresh enthusiasm to world evangelism, promote harmony and cooperation within the Church for accomplishing Christ's Great Commission, and serve as a catalyst for new evangelistic efforts and further equip younger leaders for evangelism around the world."

LCWE Chairman, Leighton Ford, stated that the purpose of the conference would be to strategize and take advantage of new opportunities for world evangelism.

According to a May 1989 article in *Decision*, approximately 50 percent of the participants will be from the Third World, half will be under forty-five, and 25 percent will be women.

Evidences for Global Revival

Jesus said, "You shall know the truth and the truth shall set you free." Perhaps the best cure for the New World Order and totalitarianism is revival. People who have come into a saving knowledge of Jesus Christ are not candidates for propaganda and enslaving ideologies.

All across the globe there is evidence of revival according to the *National and International Religion Report* whose editor is Ed Plowman. The report keeps an excellent pulse on what is happening around the globe. The following information is evidence of revival.

Here in the United States, evangelist Greg Laurie

preached to a summer crowd of ninety thousand people
jammed into and around the Pacific Amphitheater. The
amphitheater only seats eighteen thousand. A reported five
thousand people accepted Jesus Christ. The mega-event,
which dwarfed most rock concerts, was basically ignored
by the media. Greg Laurie is the pastor of the nine thousand
member Harvest Christian Fellowship, an outgrowth of
Calvary Chapel of Costa Mesa. Laurie spoke on prophecy
and the Middle East crisis.

Afterward, thousands of young people thronged to the
beaches at Corona del Mar for a mass baptism under the
direction of Pastor Chuck Smith of Calvary Chapel. Smith
likened the overwhelming response to the Jesus movement
ocean baptisms reported in *Time* and *Newsweek* over a
decade earlier.

At the Hoosier Dome twenty-four thousand charis-
matics from all denominations gathered for the North
American Congress on the Holy Spirit and World Evangelism, organized by Vinson Synan and a team of
Christians from diverse denominations. Attendees at the
conference prayed for the world's 935 million Moslems
under the direction of Joy Dawson and heard a variety of
speakers covering a wide range of subjects.

The Southern Baptist Churches launched a "Here's
Hope" evangelistic campaign in 22,500 churches with
101,000 people coming to Jesus Christ. Additional cam-
paigns brought an additional 56,323 people to Christ and
created eighty-four new congregations.

On the international scene, the Africa Inland Mission
reported that 33.1 percent of the world's population called
themselves Christians. (The goal will be to disciple these
largely nominal Christians.) *Facts* magazine reported that
there are now more evangelical Christians in Brazil than in

all of Europe, and seven churches are being birthed each day in Korea.

In Manilla, Campus Crusade for Christ (through their New Life 200 evangelistic campaign) report 91,800 converts to Jesus Christ.

In Romania, evangelist Luis Palau reports thirty-two thousand accepting Jesus Christ. Former astronaut to the moon Col. James Irwin took part in a crusade in Czechoslovakia at the Prague Sports Hall where one thousand people accepted Christ.

Episcopal evangelist John Guest reported the largest evangelistic campaign in the Soviet Union. He spoke to twelve thousand at a stadium in Gorky Park and seventeen thousand at a stadium in Kiev. Other evangelists held meetings at the Moscow Olympic Sports Palace with many thousands coming to Christ.

Campus Crusade for Christ founder, Bill Bright, has pledged one million Bibles for Soviet Christians. Through his distribution of the movie *Jesus* in the U.S.S.R., Campus Crusade announced that fifty-six thousand Soviets have seen the movie with seventy prints being distributed across Russia. On a global level, Campus Crusade for Christ reports 330 peoples worldwide have seen the *Jesus* movie that has been dubbed into 150 languages with 30 million people accepting Jesus Christ!

Reports from South Africa, Europe, China, and around the   globe indicate that a new wave of evangelism is happening.[3]

Evidences of Global Revival Continued

Billy Graham preached to crowds of more than three thousand people every night at Hong Kong stadium. Throughout Asia and the Pacific Rim (in forty-eight languages) the Graham organization trained forty-thousand counselors and printed over 10 million pieces of literature in thirty languages.

Graham said of the crusade, "In some ways, I feel that I am ready to go to heaven now . . . I have seen the greatest crusade of my life."[4]

Lifeforce

Since the Fall of man, mankind has been fighting to return to Paradise both individually and collectively.

The entire history of the human race and of the individual is an attempt to re-establish this paradise—sometimes through military or personal conquest, sometimes through spiritual force. Sexual drive, experimentation with drugs and alcohol, materialism, the various religions, and occult teachings are all attempts by man to push aside the cherubim and the flaming sword and partake of the tree of life.

However, in the universe built upon divine law, there is only one way to return to Eden and partake of the tree of life—through faith in Jesus Christ.

All of mankind's ideologies such as communism, humanism, Mohammedism, Buddhism, Hinduism, materialism, Darwinism, behaviorism, mysticism, etc., are counterfeit attempts to return man to Paradise through a way other than the cross of Jesus Christ.

In our day as never before in human history the personal saga of mankind has reached a crescendo. We are in a state of sensory overload and amplification at every level. Human history, due to the technology of nuclear warfare, ecological extinction, and computer systems, has placed the human race in a state of global jeopardy. One false move could plunge man into extinction like a set of dominoes tumbling on a card table. As such, people everywhere are looking for a power to make their lives work.

It is because of human suffering that men and women reach for answers. Consequently, we see what is termed the New Age movement and a massive social migration to Eastern religions. Millions upon millions of Westerners flock to gurus, spiritual teachers, and organizations like Werner Erhard's Transformational Technologies, Scientology, Transcendental Meditation, etc.

We see Christianity being offered with only limited acceptance on the international level. Despite the reports of global revival, international society as a whole continues to slide into a new Dark Age of mysticism and amorality. One must ask, is this lack of penetration of the Gospel of Jesus Christ into a mass culture a result of the weakness of Christ's message or rebellious mankind going past the point of no return? No! the correct analysis of mankind's current spiritual condition leads us to understand that it is not the true Gospel of Jesus Christ that is being communicated on a global level and in the United States, Europe, or the other nations of the world.

The Apostle Paul summed it up when he said, "For the Kingdom of God is not a matter of talk, but of power!" (1 Cor. 4:20). What we have seen a great deal of in our day is the Gospel of Jesus Christ relegated to the area of mere talk and not in the demonstration of power. Happily there have been many notable exceptions with salvation, healing, and revival that have happened across the globe. Yet, in too many cases the Gospel of Jesus Christ has either been reduced to mere words or the trivialization of the supernatural by superficial and sometimes dishonest people who lack both character, dimension, and intellectual as well as scriptural integrity. The net result has been a mass populace on planet Earth who have never been exposed to the real Gospel of Jesus Christ with power.

What kind of power are we talking about? We are talking about genuine supernatural power and the lifeforce of Jesus Christ as discussed in Luke 24:49 when Jesus said, "And behold, I will send forth upon you what My Father has promised; but remain in the city (Jerusalem) until you are clothed with power from on high" (Amplified Bible).

True biblical Christians are to be clothed with power from on high. Then and only then can they fulfill the Great Commission which Jesus Christ talked about in Luke 4:18-19 when he quoted from Isaiah.

> The Spirit of the Lord (is) upon Me, because he has anointed Me (the Anointed One, the Messiah) to preach the Good News (the Gospel) to the poor; He has sent Me to announce release to the captives, and recovery of sight to the blind; to send forth deliverance to those who are oppressed—who are downtrodden, bruised, crushed and broken down by calamity;
>
> To proclaim the accepted and acceptable year of the Lord—the day when salvation and the free favors of God profusely abound. (Isa. 61, Amplified)

God's infinite goodness toward man will be showered upon him through the Spirit of the Lord. In Ezekiel 34:26-27 God says, "I will cause showers to come down in their season; there shall be showers of blessing. Then the trees of the field shall yield their fruit. They shall be safe in their land; and they shall know that I am the Lord."

It is the power of God that causes blessing and the total rejuvenation of the human situation. God's lifeforce through His Spirit is a distinct and tangible force for good that enters life as we know it and changes it forever. Once biblical Christians allow this force of righteousness to permeate every aspect of their being, then they become radioactive with the love of God. This radiation of love and power affects everything around them for good.

This is the Gospel of Jesus Christ. It is a powerful supernatural force from Heaven released in the lives of believers. It is from this cleansing flow that all life emanates; this is what we call LIFEFORCE. An actual force of life emanating from God Himself.

Standing by the Roaring River of Eternity

It is primarily the appetitive nature that drives man. Unfortunately, the darkened heart of fallen man has been corrupted by the deathforce of sin. He is consumed by passion   for forbidden fruit, which manifests itself in unbridled passion for power, lust, greed, violence, etc. Man was designed to be passionate and to have his heart consumed. But fallen man, infected with the deathforce, becomes consumed with dark passions. Such is the story of the human race.

God, in all His wisdom and intelligence, designed man to be a passionate being. A person without passion is a dead person subsisting on television and tranquilizers. A person without   passion worships the idol of mediocrity and becomes like that which he or she worships. Our culture is fraught with people who have become passionless and do not worship God. They worship the idol of mediocrity upon which they have placed a little crucifix to alleviate their guilt. Those who are in darkness display more passion for their sin and rebellion than those who are in the light.

Meanwhile, a church in need of reformation moves in a perpetual state of apathy. Could it be that many have never seen the face of Jesus Christ? Could it be that they have never been transformed with a literal supernatural encounter with the living God?

The Apostle John relates the following experience.

> Then he showed me the river whose waters give life,
> sparkling crystal, flowing out from the throne of
> God and of the Lamb. Through the middle of the
> broad way of the city; also, on either side of the river
> the tree of life with its twelve varieties of fruit,
> yielding each month its fresh crop; and the leaves
> for the healing and the restoration of the nations.
> (Rev. 22:1-2, Amplified)

Standing by the river of God is a life transforming
experience. One is overcome with the roaring power of its
cleansing life. It plunges us into deep communion with the
Father. The gushing and surging torrent of the river of God
brings us to the throne room of God where we behold the
King in all His majesty. His divine presence fills us and
infuses us with life.

When we are filled with the river of life—the
LIFEFORCE—its streams can flow from us to a parched
world. It is the glory of God that can and will fight our
battles, and it is the glory of God that causes satanic
kingdoms to tumble down. God has a magnificent army
with heavenly troops eager to mobilize on our behalf. An
array of heavenly angelic forces stands waiting to deliver
us if we will but allow Him to move.

Once the dominion of God is over us, then and only
then can we extend His dominion to our world. First, we
must be under authority before we can extend the authority
and control of Christ to this dark world.

Particle Generator for an Infinite Universe

When I was in the film business, as an independent
movie producer, we used to go on location with large
portable electrical generators housed in trucks and fueled
by gasoline. This one single generator provided the

electricity for the lights on the set. In a sense, it was the power source for the entire operation.

In our universe, with its billions of twinkling stars and seemingly endless galaxies, the entire operation is powered by a massive engine with an endless source of power. Despite what some scientists claim in our day, this great engine that drives the universe is not some abstract force or energy field. The force behind the universe is the personal, living God of the universe. He is an actual person and a supreme being. The billions of suns, which burn with the massive roar of nuclear and chemical explosions, the ocean tides created by the gravitational pull of the moon, the planets revolving in planned orbits, the symphony of birds singing at sunrise, the bursting forth of the flowers in the fields in rich colors, human life growing inside the womb after the sperm and egg unite in a holy dance, the passion between married lovers and the laughter of little children all have as their source the infinite personal, living God of the universe.

It is this true God who rules from His throne in another dimension we call heaven that provides the driving force for the cosmos and all of creation. It is He and He alone who is the Author of Creation.

> And there will be no more night: they have no need for lamplight or sunlight, for the Lord God will illuminate them and be their light, and they shall reign (as kings) forever—through the eternities of eternities. (Rev. 22:5, Amplified)

The light of the universe comes from God Himself. It is a dazzling and life creating light which emanates from a Person. It is a delight to bask in the light of His magnificent presence. The Light of God has the anthem of the Lamb that was slain and resurrected from the dead to newness of life. It is light, which is produced from the blood of this

Lamb, that cleanses us from the death stain of spiritual darkness and decay. By uniting our hearts with the Lamb upon the throne, we bask in the Easter light of eternal resurrection. It is a light that transcends a billion stars and all the sunrises of earth combined. He is a glorious and supernatural light that earthly words cannot describe, and at this time, it is only our conceptional thought that can begin to conceive the dazzling glimmer of this light dawning from the sunrise of a brand new world.

A Winnable War

As I have stated throughout this book, we are moving at an alarming rate into a brave new world and a New World Order guided by a largely invisible elite. This elite is not one giant, unified conspiracy. The commonality among the conspirators emerges from their commonly held philosophy. Consequently, history flows on as a by-product of the thoughts, ideas, and philosophies of the men and women who compose human history.

The demise of our day has been precipitated by the failed ideas of men who do not understand their universe or each other. They have failed to understand their origins. We are not the children of subatomic particles. We are the children of a personal God who cares.

The chaos of our day and the quantity of human suffering has been largely manufactured by the ideas that men hold. If we are to change the course of human history and alleviate human suffering, we must strike at the root of the problem. Although petitioning, voting, political change, demonstrating, and fighting intelligently for what we believe in should be a part of every person's call, our primary thrust must be to challenge the foundational ideologies of our day with the sword of truth. Not just religious truth, but historical, sociological, medical, scientific, and psychological truth.

Our battle is a battle of ideas. We are not fighting men and women or organizations. We are fighting the strongholds of ideas and beliefs that have laid waste our generation. In the final analysis, we must rise up as an army of creative visionaries who have been transformed by an overwhelming vision of another world. A world based on an eternal kingdom. We must create (by the power of the Holy Spirit) a true Christian counterculture that can live in distinct contrast to the darkness of a secular culture that surrounds us.

The hallmark of this counterculture must be love for each other and love for mankind. Not in a sugary sweet and mystical sense. But, as agents of divine love, we must be willing to carry the cross before a dying world in the hope of winning them for Jesus Christ.

Petitions, demonstrations, television programs, and books all have their place. But a group of people, however tiny, who have a clear cut vision based on eternal principles and true love for one another can change the direction of human history.

Armies can be turned back, governments can crumble, and media empires like the empires of old can rise and fall. But a people who have been captured by a force far greater than themselves and who have been consumed by a divine vision cannot be stopped. The fires of revival and the force of true biblical reformation cannot be stopped by any government on earth.

One reason some young people have succumbed to the hedonism and rebellion of a secular age is because they have not been confronted with the Christianity of Jesus Christ. They have seen an American middle class Christian religion, which is not always the same thing as biblical

Christianity. What is needed in our day is not more programs, petitions, or meetings. It is not more books, evangelistic crusades, or speakers. What is needed is the divine impartation of a burning vision of God.

The founders of the early church were ordinary fishermen, tax collectors, etc. They were completely transformed by encountering Jesus Christ. In the power of that transformation, they turned civilization upside down. The religious establishment and the full force of the Roman government could not stop the spread of the Gospel of Jesus Christ and its impact upon the world.

In our day, as we witness the decline of civilization and the dawn of a new Dark Age, we have not been left alone in the battle. We are not to stand fatalistically and watch the destruction of our generation. We have been given the powers of the kingdom of heaven. We can face the tidal wave of secular destruction as Moses confronted the Red Sea. With the same power that enabled Moses to hold back the sea from crushing the children of Israel, we can hold back the waters of destruction in our day.

In order to do that, we must completely reject the sins of isolationism, retreatism, and apathy that have plagued the Christian culture. We must press forward while there is still time. We must grasp hold of Christ and His cross until our hands bruise and bleed. As we surrender our fears and humanness before the Lord of history, we will see not only his triumphant return but the triumph of His kingdom.

Who Will Lead the Culture?

On one hand you have those of the humanistic and Eastern mystical perspective producing a powerful, creative, and intellectual force. It has diligently grabbed the helm of the great ship of modern civilization and chartered a course toward an illusive utopia. It will ultimately take up port on the island of Chaos. On the other hand, you have a primarily pietistic evangelical culture that affirms the Scripture to some degree but has not produced creative, moral, and political leadership. It has lost control of the direction of the culture through default.

In contrast, except for a relatively small number of exceptions, those who hold a Judeo-Christian world view are rather small in number when it comes to a rich tradition in science, art, and culture. This was not always so. In previous generations the great thinkers and artists were often those with a Judeo-Christian world view. One thinks of William Shakespeare, C.S. Lewis, Mozart, Bach, Handel, Michelangelo, Winston Churchill, Isaac Newton, Blaise Pascal and thousands of others. In fact, modern science was built by men like Sir Isaac Newton, Robert Boyle, and Blaise Pascal.

Some who have assumed the role of leadership and who speak for the biblical world view sometimes come from a very flat and one dimensional spectrum of life. They have no real intellectual or moral authority in our society because they are speaking out of a wind tunnel of empty pietism. Their stance of noninvolvement (politically, socially, culturally) is scripturally indefensible. They have, by their silence, told the secular humanists to "take control of society." Therefore, they cannot comment on movies because they do not understand movies. They cannot comment about art, except in terms of censorship, because they do not know anything about art. They cannot comment about science, because they do not understand science and so on. Those who speak for the Judeo-Christian view in our culture—many of those who have assumed control of electronic pulpits—are often not equipped to be cultural leaders because they know nothing about the culture.

In stark contrast, the biblical prophets like Joseph and

Daniel (highly educated and respected) gave practical solutions to their societies concerning economics, world hunger, and so on. They were listened to by the pagan cultures who acknowledged their God because they were convicted by their wisdom.

The Heart of the Matter

The basic issue facing our culture and the world in general is the question, "What is final reality?" In other words, what world view is really correct concerning our universe, world, and culture? This is the heart of the matter.

The basic issue is not such things as pornography, drugs, abortion, trilateralism, the occult, divorce, crime, globalism, censorship, euthanasia, the Constitution or whatever. It is true these are all vitally important issues. But, they are peripheral to the central issue.

The real question is "What is final reality?" Do we indeed live in a universe where human life is the result of random chance as men like Charles Darwin or Carl Sagan believe?

Or is there a real personal, living God of the universe as the Old Testament and New Testament reveal? The question is not whether or not 50 million people claim to believe in Jesus Christ in America. This means nothing. Fifty million people used to believe the world was flat until Christopher Columbus sailed over the seas. More than fifty million people believe that Mohammed is God's prophet. Numbers prove nothing. Truth has never been the product of a popular vote because what is true is not always popular. The question must be asked, "Which world view is correct?"

The abortion protests and the whole issue of the sanctity of life, the concept of monogamous and heterosexual marriage, pornography, the civil rights of men and women, globalism and democracy emerge from a world view. Either, a biblical world view that acknowledges the absolutes of a personal God, or an Eastern mystical world view that has its roots in Hinduism, or a secular humanist world view that believes there is no God—only energy plus chance.

Men and women act in accordance with some belief system. To fight only peripheral battles, no matter how important they might be, without attacking the fundamental issue of a world view will not solve the problem.

The problem in our society is millions of people, especially among the educated and the elite, are absolutely convinced that the Judeo-Christian world view is an anachronism. These people are convinced that the universe is all there is. They believe man is the center of the universe and that all of us are here as the result of an evolutionary explosion.

When this humanistic society looks upon both conservative Jews, Protestants, or Catholics, they view this Judeo-Christian culture as a kind of throwback to the Dark Ages. They perceive us as terribly misinformed. They think that what we believe flies in the face of the so-called scientific evidence.

As such, they perceive themselves as the "enlightened ones." They seek to adopt a parental role toward society. They begin to radically re-construct society based upon a humanistic blue print. If we are the product of evolution and there is no real personal God why not abort babies, have homosexual relationships, practice mercy killing of the elderly, or create a global government ruled by a scientific elite? If there is no Creator, Author, or Designer, why not invent the rules as we go along?

The key issue that affects those with a Judeo-Christian world view is one of confronting a culture that is hostile to truth. The peripheral battles will continue to rage and intensify as long as this problem of world view and final reality is not dealt with.

As we approach the new millennium and confront openly a post-Christian culture, we must ask ourselves why this culture is so convinced that there is no personal God. Is it because they have not seen evidence to the contrary because the Church of Jesus Christ has not been the visible witness of the truth in our time that it should be?

Among the elite there are many who have deliberately chosen to reject the truth. Yet, there are millions more in all levels of society who have not been confronted with an adequate apologetic. They have not been truly evangelized because they have often seen a non-biblical, shallow, and superficial Church that does not stand for final reality.

The key therefore in reaching these people is not to simply battle them on peripheral issues. It is to challenge their world view with the truth in a compelling manner that is spiritually credible and intellectually honest. Christianity that practices super spirituality, isolationism, and retreatism has no real power to confront a hostile culture.

What is needed is nothing less than both revival and Reformation, or to use stronger words: a revolution in the thinking of those who hold a Judeo-Christian world view so that truth can be adequately presented and lived before a spiritually alienated culture. There are multiplied millions who have seen "religion" and unreality and a lack of love from the Church and they have fled from it. They have rejected not the truth of Christ but a contemporary religious system built on psuedo-spiritual values. They have instead embraced humanism and the deception of Eastern mystical beliefs. One has only to think of the powerful growth of an organization like Alcoholics Anonymous, which has provided an opportunity for people to get sober and be "real" with other people. The Church in its religiosity has not provided that same space. Jesus Christ ate dinner with prostitutes, tax collectors, and all kinds of people in a real setting.

Therefore to effect a major change in the direction our culture is going, a major change must first occur in the Church. History has shown us that when a society or culture begins to rot, it could be because the salt has lost its savor. The Church is in need of both revival and reformation.

Truth is so compelling and powerful that no philosophy, system, organization, or ideology can stand in its way. What is needed in our day is the birth of an authentic Judeo-Christian counterculture where Christianity once again becomes truth and not a religion.

When we, as individual Christians, allow the Lord of the universe to birth both revival and Reformation in our hearts, a powerful transformation occurs. A transformation not based on religious gymnastics. In our fleshly natures we are all sinners. There is no getting around it. But, when we cease trying to work ourselves into acceptance with God and through faith in Christ's power make room for an inner transformation to happen, then the life force of the Holy Spirit begins to flow in and out of our hearts through the Church into the culture where powerful transformation occurs.

People are desperately seeking such a vital breakthrough and powerful transformation in their lives. They have sought out compelling counterfeits of transformation such as Est, Scientology, TM, human potential programs, etc. Why have they not found this power and wonder in the Church? Why are the words of these often mystical human potential groups filled with magical words like breakthrough, transformation, commitment, love and power? They have stolen the language of redemption that rightfully belongs to the Church.

Oh, that as a Christian culture we would stop looking backward and smothering the indescribable beauty of our Savior. We must begin to look upon the face of a living Christ just as Moses looked upon the face of God. Then our faces would be transformed and shine with the eternal transforming power of God.

The transforming power of Jesus Christ can do what we through our own human engineering cannot do. It is possible to see the course of Western civilization and our culture changed in response to true revival and Reformation.

The prevailing delusion of secular humanism, mysticism, and materialism that so grip and dominate our culture will disintegrate under the rule of the kingdom of Heaven. If we say in our hearts that this is impossible, we do not understand the God of history. Who would have thought it possible to see the Berlin wall tumble down or the fall of communism in our day?

When the life force of Jesus Christ begins to move powerfully out of individual hearts that have been revived, then a Church that has been reformed produces both a quiet revolution and cultural transformation.

It must be remembered that in the darkest hours of history God's glory has shown the brightest. So too in our time, a sovereign, living God will respond to the prayers of His people and move with absolute power and force into the midst of a culture. The hallmarks of such a move of God will be genuine repentance, revival, and societal transformation.

Endnotes

Chapter One

1. Alvin Toffler, *The Third Wave* (New York: William Morrow, 1980), 25.

2. Fritjof Capra, *The Turning Point* (New York: Bantam Books, 1982), 41.

3. Suzanna Andrews, "America's Most Powerful Businessman," *Manhattan, Inc.* (May 1990): 63.

4. Walter Truett Anderson, *To Govern Evolution. Further Adventures of the Political Animal* (Orlando: Harcourt Brace Jovanovich, Inc., 1987), 252-257.

5. Ibid., 262.

6. William E. Halal, Alexander I. Nikitin, "Democratic Fire Enterprise" *Futurist* (Nov.-Dec. 1990): 14.

7. Wayne Dyer, *You'll See It When You Believe It* (New York: William Morrow Co., 1989), 94.

8. Aldous Huxley, *Brave New World Revisited* (New York: Harper and Row, 1958), 3.

9. Ibid., 137.

10. Francis Schaeffer, *The Complete Works of Francis Schaeffer*, vol. 5 (Westchester, Il.: Crossway Books, 1976), 243-244.

Chapter Two

1. Sidney Piburn, ed. and comp., *The Dalai Lama—A Policy of Kindness* (Ithaca, N.Y.: Snow Lion, 1990).

2. Alvin Toffler, *The Third Wave*, (New York: William Morrow, 1980), 342.

3. Holly Sklar, ed., *Trilateralism—The Trilateral Commission and Elite Planning for World Management* (Boston: South End Press, 1980), 3.

4. Jeff Frieden, *Trilateralism* (n.p., n.d.), 69.

5. Ben H. Bagdikian, *The Media Monopoly* (Boston: Beacon Press, 1983), 23.

6. David Shaw, "Abortion Bias Sweeps into the News," *Los Angeles Times* (July 1990):1.

7. Francis Schaeffer, *The Complete Works of Francis Schaeffer* (Westchester, Il.: Crossway Books, 1976).

8. Robert H. Bork, *The Tempting of America—The Political Seduction of the Law* (New York: The Free Press/MacMillan, 1990), 323.

9. Ibid., 9.

10. John Lippman, *Los Angeles Times* (18 May 1990)

11. Dennis Hunt, "Feminine Porn Finds a Niche in Marketplace," *Los Angeles Times* (18 May 1990): 17.

Chapter Three

1. In antiquity this error is attributable to Anaxagoras, Democritus, and the Atomists.

2. Robert Ornstein and Paul Ehrlich, *New World New Mind* (New York: Doubleday, 1989), 242-243.

3. Richard Alpert, *Remember Be Here Now* (Albuquerque: Laura Foundation, 1971).

4. Charles P. Conn, "A Young Generation at Risk," *Charisma* (Sept. 1990): 92.

Chapter Four

1. Dr. Judith A. Reisman and Edward Eichel, *Kinsey, Sex and Fraud* (Lafayette, La.: Huntington House/Lochinvar Inc., 1990).

Chapter Five

1. Ronald Brownstein, "Do Voter's Numbers Matter," *Los Angeles Times* (n.d.): 18.

Chapter Six

1. Jonathon Mann, "AIDS—The Next Ten Years," *Newsweek* (25 June 1990).

2. Russell Chandler, "Persian Gulf Crisis Stirs Predictions of Final Conflict," *Los Angeles Times* (n.d.): A5

3. Christopher Manes, *Green Rage—Radical Environmentalism and the Unmasking of Civilization* (Boston, Toronto, London: Little, Brown and Co., 1990).

4. Ibid., 142.

5. Carl Sagan, *Cosmos* (New York: Random House, 1980).

6. Ibid., 329, 331.

7. Derek Williams, "Mission Takes Off by Satellite," *Decision* (May 1989): 18.

8. Ibid., 20.

9. Joshua Levine, "The Last Gasp of the Media," *Forbes* (17 Sept. 1990).

10. Russell Chandler, "Angelenos Are Less Likely to Go to Church," *Los Angeles Times* (15 Sept. 1990): 16.

Chapter Eight

1. Pat Robertson, *Perspective* (July-Aug. 1990).

2. Loren Cunningham, "Fulfilling the Great Commission," *Charisma* (Aug. 1990): 58.

3. Data on global revival from National & International Religion Report

4. *Los Angeles Times*—Times Wire Services (24 Nov. 1990): 19.

MORE GOOD BOOKS FROM HUNTINGTON HOUSE PUBLISHERS

Cover of Darkness (A Novel)
by J. Carroll

Jack's time is running out. The network's top investigative reporter has been given the most bizarre and difficult assignment of his life. The powers behind the conspiracy (occult and demonic forces) are finally exposed by Jack. Now comes the real challenge—convincing others. Matching wits with supernatural forces, Jack faces the most hideous conspiracy the world has ever known.

ISBN 0-910311-31-5 $7.95

The Image of the Ages
by David Webber

Are the secular humanists' plans for a New World Order about to be realized? How will the establishment of this order affect you and your family? David Webber, author of *The Image of the Ages*, explains how modern technology, artificial intelligence, and other scientific advances will be used in the near future to manipulate and control the masses.

ISBN 0-910311-38-2 $7.95

Kinsey, Sex and Fraud: The Indoctrination of a People
by Dr. Judith A. Reisman and Edward Eichel

Kinsey, Sex and Fraud describes the research of Alfred Kinsey, which shaped Western society's beliefs and understanding of the nature of human sexuality. His unchallenged conclusions are taught at every level of education—elementary, high school and college—and quoted in textbooks as undisputed truth.

The authors clearly demonstrate that Kinsey's research involved illegal experimentations on several hundred children. The survey was carried out on a non-representative group of Americans, including disproportionately large numbers of sex offenders, prostitutes, prison inmates, and exhibitionists.

ISBN 0-910311-20-X $19.95 Hardcover

Lord! Why Is My Child A Rebel?
by Jacob Aranza

This book presents an analysis of the root causes of teenage rebellion and offers practical solutions for disoriented parents. Aranza focuses on the turbulent teenage years, and how to survive those years—must reading for parents—especially for those with strong-willed children. This book will help you avoid the trap in which many parents are caught.

ISBN 0-910311-62-5 $6.95

New Age Messiah Identified: Who Is Lord Maitreya?
by Troy Lawrence

Years of groping through obscure files and secret memos in a desperate attempt
to identify the New Age Messiah has finally paid off. Former New Age initiate
(Theosophist) Troy Lawrence experiences a stunning conversion to Christianity.
Although employed by the Tara Center—a major headquarters of the New Age
movement—Lawrence conceals his conversion to Christianity while feverishly
gathering vital information from one of the nerve centers of New Age activity.

ISBN 0-910311-17-X $8.95

Psychic Phenomena Unveiled: Confessions of a New Age Warlock
by John Anderson

He walked on hot coals and stopped his heart. As one of Los Angeles' most
recognized psychics, John Anderson was on top of the world. His ability to
perform psychic phenomena converted the most stubborn unbeliever into a true
believer in occult power. But John Anderson sensed his involvement in the
occult was destroying him. This book was written to expose the trickery behind
the New Age magic and address man's attraction to the occult.

ISBN 0-910311-49-8 $8.95

"Soft Porn" Plays Hardball
by Dr. Judith A. Reisman

In her second book the author clearly demonstrates that pornography imposes
on society a view of women and children that encourages violence and sexual
abuse. As crimes against women and children increase to alarming proportions,
it's of paramount importance that we recognize the cause of this violence.
Pornography should be held accountable for the havoc it has wreaked in our
homes and our country.

ISBN 0-910311-65-X $8.95 Trade paper
ISBN 0-910311-92-7 $16.95 Hardcover

New World Order: The Ancient Plan of Secret Societies
by William T. Still

For thousands of years, secret societies have cultivated an ancient plan which
has powerfully influenced world events. Until now, this secret plan has
remained hidden from view. This book presents new evidence that a military
take-over of the U.S. was considered by some in the administration of one of
our recent presidents. Although averted, the forces behind it remain in secretive
positions of power.

ISBN 0-910311-64-1 $8.95

To Grow By Storybook (Phonics) Readers
by Janet Friend

Today, the quality of education is a major concern, consequently more and more parents have turned to home schooling to teach their children how to read. The *TO GROW BY STORYBOOK READERS* by Janet Friend can greatly enhance your home schooling reading program. The set of phonics readers consists of 18 Storybook Readers plus 2 Activity Books. Although designed to be used in conjunction with Marie LeDoux's PLAY 'N TALK phonics program they will work well with any orderly phonics programs. Upon completion of the series, your child will have learned over 30 different morals, lessons, and over 50 different phonics word drills in story form.

ISBN 0-910311-69-2 $44.95 Slipcased Set

The Deadly Deception
by Tom McKenney

For the first time the 33d degree ritual is made public! Learn of the "secrets" and "deceptions" that are practiced daily around the world. Find out why Freemasonry teaches that it is the true religion, that all other religions are but corrupted and perverted forms of Freemasonry. If you know anyone in the Masonic movement, you must read this book.

ISBN 0-910311-54-4 $7.95

Seduction of the Innocent Revisited
by John Fulce

If you haven't picked up a comic book in a few years, you're in for a real shock! Today's comics are filled with obscene images, occult symbols, and even nudity. There are no more heroes battling the forces of evil. A constant anti-Christian theme similar to the anti-Semitic theme found in German literature during the 1920s and 30s should alarm even the casual observer.

ISBN 0-910311-66-8 $8.95

From Rock to Rock
by Eric Barger

Contains the first Music Rating System classifying 1500 groups and artists. The author details the path of destruction the rock music industry has followed. Includes the use of occult symbols and violent lyrics by today's groups. Twenty years of experience coupled with years of research make the author an expert in this field. Guaranteed to open the eyes and ears of all who read it.

ISBN 0-910311-61-7 $8.95

ORDER THESE BOOKS FROM HUNTINGTON HOUSE PUBLISHERS!

—— America Betrayed—Marlin Maddoux — — — — $6.95 ——
——•Cover of Darkness—J. Carroll — — — — — — — 7.95 ——
—— Deadly Deception: Freemasonry—Tom McKenney—— 7.95 ——
—— Delicate Balance—John Zajac — — — — — — — 8.95 ——
—— Devil Take The Youngest—Winkie Pratney — — — 8.95 ——
—— The Devil's Web—Pat Pulling/K. Cawthon — — — — 8.95 ——
—— Dinosaurs and the Bible—Dave Unfred — — — — 12.95 ——
——•En Route to Global Occupation—James Meredith —— 8.95 ——
—— Exposing the AIDS Scandal—Dr. Paul Cameron —— — 7.95 ——
—— From Rock to Rock—Eric Barger— — — — — — 8.95 ——
—— God's Rebels—Henry Lee Curry III, Ph.D. — — — — 12.95 ——
—— Hidden Dangers of the Rainbow—Constance Cumbey — 8.95 ——
——•The Image of the Ages—David Webber — — — — 7.95 ——
—— Inside the New Age Nightmare—Randall Baer — — — 8.95 ——
—— Jubilee on Wall Street—David Knox Barker— — — 7.95 ——
——•Kinsey, Sex and Fraud—Dr. Judith A. Reisman &
                    Edward Eichel   Hard cover —— 19.95 ——
—— Last Days Collection—Last Days Ministries — — — 8.95 ——
——•Lord! Why Is My Child A Rebel?—Jacob Aranza — — 6.95 ——
—— Lucifer Connection—Joseph Carr — — — — — — 7.95 ——
——•New Age Messiah Identified—Troy Lawrence — — — 8.95 ——
—— New World Order: The Ancient Plan of Secret Societies—
                     William T. Still — — — 8.95 ——
—— Personalities in Power—Florence Littauer   — — — 8.95 ——
——•Psychic Phenomena Unveiled—John Anderson — — 8.95 ——
—— Seduction of the Innocent Revisited—John Fulce— — 8.95 ——
——•Soft Porn Plays Hardball—Dr. Judith A. Reisman— —
                     Trade paper — — — 8.95 ——
                     Hard cover — — — — 16.95 ——
—— To Grow By Storybook Readers—Janet Friend   44.95 per set ——
—— Twisted Cross—Joseph Carr — — — — — — — 8.95 ——
——•Who Will Rule the Future?—Paul McGuire — — — 8.95 ——
                     Shipping and Handling   ——
                     TOTAL   ——

•New Titles

AVAILABLE AT BOOKSTORES EVERYWHERE or order direct from:
Huntington House Publishers • P.O. Box 53788 • Lafayette, LA 70505
Send check/money order. For faster service use VISA/MASTERCARD, call
toll-free 1-800-749-4009
Add: Freight and handling, $3.00 for the first book ordered, and $.50 for each
additional book up to 5 books.

Enclosed is $ _____ including postage.
Card type: _____
VISA/MASTERCARD# _____ Exp. Date ——
Name _____
Address _____
City, State, Zipcode _____